PENGUIN BOOKS

INSPIRING ORGANICS

INSPIRING ORGANICS

HEALTHY FOOD BALANCE FOR MIND, BODY AND SOUL

David Clark

Photography by Patrick Reynolds

Penguin

PENGUIN BOOKS

Penguin Books (NZ) Ltd, cnr Airborne and Rosedale Roads, Albany,
Auckland 1310, New Zealand
Penguin Books Ltd, 27 Wrights Lane, London W8 5TZ, England
Penguin Putnam Inc, 375 Hudson Street, New York, NY 10014, United States
Penguin Books Australia Ltd, 487 Maroondah Highway,
Ringwood, Australia 3134
Penguin Books Canada Ltd, 10 Alcorn Avenue, Toronto,
Ontario, Canada M4V 3B2
Penguin Books (South Africa) Pty Ltd, 5 Watkins Street,
Denver Ext 4, 2094, South Africa
Penguin Books India Ltd, 11, Community Centre, Panchsheel Park,
New Delhi 110 017, India
Penguin Books Ltd, Registered Offices: Harmondsworth, Middlesex, England

First published by Penguin Books (NZ) Ltd, 2000

1 3 5 7 9 10 8 6 4 2

Copyright © text, David Clark 2000
Copyright © photography, Patrick Reynolds 2000

The right of David Clark to be identified as the author of this work in terms of section 96 of the
Copyright Act 1994 is hereby asserted.

Designed by Dexter Fry and Lorraine Still
Typeset by Egan-Reid Ltd
Printed in Hong Kong by Condor Production Ltd

ISBN 0 14 029876 2

Special thanks to Eon Art Design Espresso, Republic Home and Chris from Atomic Café, Balmoral.

www.penguin.com

CONTENTS

DEDICATION

First and foremost, my sincere gratitude to the many students and clients with inspired, valuable insights who have encouraged me to share my knowledge, so that they may have an ongoing reminder of the means and ways to fully experience the healthy lifestyle they are already enjoying and so truly deserve.

Secondly, I dedicate this book to you, the reader, that you too may receive the vision of my dream and be inspired to listen with an open mind to my simple philosophy and experience the satisfaction of nurturing yourself with a lifestyle that allows your body to do as nature intended – to constantly rejuvenate and heal in its own natural rhythm and flow.

ACKNOWLEDGEMENTS

Thank you, Mum, for believing in me, and Dad, for always being there; and Paul and John, my brothers, for the wisdom you have shared. Thank you, Kris, my son – you make my life complete. Andrew Krukziener, your optimistic flair has encouraged me so much to persist and see solutions. David Muller, you are my mentor and you have kept me focused. Dr Helen Gurr, you showed me that there is never only one way of doing things. Monica Reeves, my catechism teacher of eight years, thank you for sharing your faith – through you I could believe in myself, in others, and in life. Michelle Nicol, my sweetheart for 15 years, wife for eight years, and mother of Kris, thank you for persisting with change, when in my earlier years of study your determined nature often led the way. My thanks to Ray Ridolfi, my shiatsu teacher. Wataru Ohashi, our master, your smile embraced my soul. Montse and Peter Bradford – I know I was a tough student, but from you both I learned well and often recall the food, times and experiences that we all shared at Balneth Manor. Thank you Mark and Dianna Newcomb for your spiritual aspirations. Steven Fisher, it is through your integrity in life that I know values. Brian Joyce, your depth of character, wit and knowledge have given me direction – as you put it, 'stick to your knitting'. Charles Richard-Worth, my uncle and organic farmer, in my youth you took me to the land. Thank you Lee Parore and Emile Palmer, for without friends where would we be? Your strengths have helped me fly. Anita Blanchet, the poetry and art we have shared is special and divine. And of course Mauna Palmdetto from Italy, we have touched the highest peak and spoken through our truths. I thank you all for simply being there. I'd like to remember Nick Kerkham. My dear friend Nick, although you are no longer with us, my wild canoeing friend, you and I together have done time, and in the wildness of the rivers, we played and carved our way.

Thank you also to Patrick Reynolds and Maria Majsa for your creative input and for opening your home for the making of this book.

DAVID'S STORY

At the heart of my life and work is a deep understanding that food is fundamental to health and wellbeing.

As a teenager I was plagued with severe shin-splints despite being an extremely competitive white-water kayaker, racing slalom at national level. At times I was in such debilitating pain that it was unbearable. It was difficult for me to walk and near impossible to run. I visited many specialists at the time who prescribed various techniques and mechanical supports, but nothing really helped. At its worst, I was told there was nothing that could be done for me. One specialist informed me: 'There is nothing we can do and if it continues like this you will probably be in a wheelchair by the time you are 40.'

Given the severity of the prognosis I began exploring outside the mainstream medical world for new ways to fix my legs. At 18 I travelled to a spiritual gathering in the South Island and while there met an Ananda Maga priest who taught me about food, meditation and yoga. I was truly inspired. I changed my diet, meditated and did yoga daily and within three months the leg pains had completely disappeared.

In 1983 I travelled to London and studied at the British School of Shiatsu and the London Kushi Macrobiotic Institute. I graduated in 1986 and spent the following year working in a macrobiotic community in Southern England, at the same time establishing my own shiatsu practice in Brighton. During this time I was also privileged to work with the most experienced shiatsu and macrobiotic masters in the world. I am profoundly indebted to those life-changing experiences.

I eventually moved back to London and set up a private practice. A short while later I was offered the opportunity to do medicinal cooking for wealthy private clients. One well-known client was the comedian Terry Thomas, who was by then very sick with Parkinson's disease. I visited him daily at his home, preparing all his meals, and gave him shiatsu massage.

I returned to New Zealand in November 1988. The following February I established the New Zealand School of Shiatsu in Queen Street, Auckland, teaching shiatsu and macrobiotic cooking. In 1989 I extended the business to incorporate a shiatsu beauty therapy clinic.

From 1988 to 1994 I taught over 5000 people about organic food, health and wellbeing. The school became a foundation of support committed to teaching and inspiring others to explore their own potential for happiness and wellbeing.

However, while the business flourished, I was becoming increasingly frustrated at being unable to recommend reliable sources of high-quality organic food. At the time, only 0.5 per cent of New Zealand produce was organically grown, supply networks of organic food were limited, and many of my clients were simply unable to obtain organic food. I realised that things needed to change. Organic Home Delivery was established in 1996 in response to that need. It was the right time for the business: at the end of my first year I was supplying 250 homes with organic foods.

Organic foods are now available in many supermarkets and health food stores. The number of hectares producing organic food nationwide has doubled over the last few years to meet consumer demand.

Given my deep belief that organic food is a foundation building-block for lifelong good health, it is my aim to increase awareness of organic foods and their healing properties, especially for our children. Too many of our children are eating junk food. At the same time we are seeing burgeoning rates of ill-health. I believe it is time to inspire a new generation about food balance and organics – for the sake of our children and our future.

I am passionate about how foods affect body tone, health and vitality.

During the two decades that I've been both student and practitioner of macrobiotics and shiatsu massage, I've seen many people transform their lives – skin problems have cleared, weight has been lost, and people have experienced vastly improved energy levels and relief from many serious illnesses such as cancer, liver disorders and irritable bowel syndrome.

I believe that inner balance is brought about through the consumption of seasonal, organic, natural foods. If you avoid toxic chemicals by eating organic food, you will enjoy greater levels of health and vitality.

Throughout this book you will learn how foods affect your body.

IN THE BEGINNING – THE FOUR-LEVEL PROCESS

Energy can be neither created nor destroyed, only changed from one form to another. That is, every manifestation, physical or non-physical, is a constantly changing form. This book describes how food energy changes to body energy, or more simply, how food qualities affect body form, whether that be how you look, feel or function.

Change is one of the most basic and profound elements of life. Each and every manifestation of life – from molecules to cells, to skin, to the shape of your body – is constantly changing, and if you want to be in control of your body and to affect its tone, youthfulness and vitality, you must understand how food energy converts to body energy.

Food is our life's blood. 'You are what you eat', and the quality of what you eat is essential to create high levels of energy. Organic food is crucial to the quality and essence of our blood, our wellbeing and our lives.

Organic plants supply vitamins and minerals essential to our wellbeing. They also contain other imperceptible qualities such as the ability to burn fat, eliminate fluids, rejuvenate, purify, strengthen and heal our bodies.

I've spent 15 years creating a simple and workable four-level process using foods that will give you more energy and balance in your day-to-day life. This involves using foods that have energising, cleansing, strengthening and toning qualities.

ENERGISING
Energising foods activate cell vitality. When every cell in the body is energised, you feel more alive. Energising foods are predominantly foods that are high in enzymes and 'good' bacteria that aid rejuvenation. *(See p. 25)*

CLEANSING
Cleansing foods eliminate toxins from your blood. These foods are fruit, vegetables and seaweeds, prepared in a way that helps rid your body of the chemicals and toxins that cause sluggish metabolic activity. *(See p. 37)*

STRENGTHENING
Strengthening foods bring elasticity and resilience to your cells. They build immune strength and provide your body with power. Strengthening foods are the protein foods – beans, pulses, legumes and fish, which bring a vitality to your body that you can measure. *(See p. 59)*

TONING

Toning foods complete the cycle of change. The contractual qualities of grains tone the cells. Grains have incredible abilities to pull energy into the core. Such grains include rice, barley, millet, oats, quinoa and amaranth. *(See p. 81)*

NATURE AND BALANCE

The four levels reflect a balance found throughout nature.

Spring energy is rising and stimulates growth and activity – these qualities are similar to the **energising** foods.

Summer energy is outward energy that brings the fullness of summer alive with leaf and flower – these qualities are similar to the convectional qualities of the **cleansing** foods.

Autumn energy brings forth the gathering qualities of inward energy that cause fruit to ripen and leaves to fall – these qualities are similar to the **strengthening** foods that pull energy into and enliven the cells.

Winter energy is deep; it contracts life force within the living plant – such qualities are similar to **toning** foods, which focus energy and vitality within the body.

The four levels of eating are like nature – they flow in balance.

SEASONAL FOODS

In days gone by everyone ate in harmony with nature – rich hardy root vegetables such as pumpkin, carrots, kumara and potato in the winter and lighter salad vegetables such as beans, corn, tomatoes, courgettes and lettuce in summer. Eating in balance with nature allows our bodies to flow in harmony with the greater cycles of life.

The winter fruit and vegetables are essential for our winter balance. These foods have a more inward or contractual energy, and work to increase our body temperature and build immunity for the winter months. These strong vegetables help to combat colds, flu and fatigue.

Summer heat produces a lighter, quicker growth of vegetables and fruits that are essential for summer balance. These foods are cleansing and purifying as this season has a lighter, more outward energy that transports heat out of the body and keeps it cool. Hence winter foods build immune strength and summer foods purify the body: this is balance.

However, the advent of refrigeration, air transport and canned foods over the last 100 years has seen a radical change in the way we eat. Processed foods now make up the bulk of our diet and we have become adept at eating out-of-season fruit and vegetables all year round.

While this may appear a bonus for consumer choice, it leaves our bodies in a seriously confused and unbalanced state. Eating tropical bananas or out-of-season apricots on a cold winter's day chills the body down and places stress on the system. So wide has our food choice become that many people no longer actually know what is in season.

Organic fruit and vegetables have a shorter season than conventionally-grown produce because organic foods are grown using natural methods. But the bonus is that foods in season taste as they should – juicy and flavoursome.

GETTING STARTED

I'm certain that reading this book will excite and inspire you as to the possibilities of how good you can look and feel. Here are some key points to get you results.

1. GO ORGANIC

Substitute the foods you are currently eating for organic food. By removing chemicals and toxins from your body and eating foods that are grown in a natural soil environment, you will immediately begin the process of change that will help you look and feel stronger.

2. EXPERIMENT

Throughout this book there are many exciting recipes for you to try. Begin introducing them gradually alongside your current meals. For example, try replacing your normal lettuce and tomato salad with a high-enzyme pressed salad with its amazing antioxidising qualities. Try using miso paste or shoyu instead of other flavourings that are chemical based.

3. THREE DAYS

Try introducing the four-level process for three concurrent days each week. Then eat as you normally do for the rest of the week. Just three days a week is enough to give your body time to start rejuvenating its cells.

4. GO FOR GOLD

Organic food is nutritionally more valuable. The four-level process is a healthy, balanced way of providing you with proteins, carbohydrates, fresh vegetables and fruit. Share your excitement about this way of eating with family and friends. Show off your new culinary skills. You'll be amazed at how many people enjoy the pleasure of seasonal organic food balance.

5. HAVE FUN!

This book is designed to give you the foundation of balance and the power to create vitality for your body. But allow yourself the pleasure of eating foods you enjoy just for fun.

Listen to your body. There are times when you crave certain foods – enjoy them. I believe you'll create the foundation of balance by focusing on the positive aspects of the new organic foods you are eating. A balanced diet with an element of fun is far superior to a rigid diet with an element of guilt.

WHY ORGANIC?

Is there a choice? Are we debating the use of chemical sprays as opposed to natural farming methods, or synthetic fertilisers as opposed to organic composting methods? I don't believe there is a debate.

Research shows that exposure to pesticides significantly reduces the number of white blood cells and disease-fighting lymphocytes, thus making you significantly more vulnerable to disease. By simply eating 'fresh' non-organic produce, millions of people are exposing themselves to poisonous pesticides, 90 per cent of which are carcinogenic. Most importantly, only organic food is guaranteed to be totally free of genetic modification – the artificial manipulation of plant and animal cells.

WHAT IS ORGANIC FARMING?

Organic farming involves the rotation of crops so that the soil does not become exhausted or vulnerable to disease as occurs with large-scale one-crop conventional farming.

Organic food is grown in rich humus, soil that is high in organic matter and powerful in life-sustaining energy. This creates a nutritionally-alive crop essential for building a solid foundation of health.

Organic farming methods focus on healthy soil which is valued for its ability to grow healthy plants. Healthy soil is like the immune system of the body – when it is in balance, the plants growing in it are strong. When the plants are strong, they fight off the disease and bacteria that most conventional farmers use chemical sprays against.

Organic farmers avoid applying any artificial chemicals to their plants or soil, or feeding any growth hormones or antibiotics to their animal stock.

Science is now proving what organic farmers have long believed: comparative studies between 'pure organic' farming and 'conventional' farming clearly illustrate a higher mineral content in organically grown produce.

Because there are no residues from growth hormones, fertilisers or sprays to harm you, organic foods are healthier for you and your family. And organic foods taste as food should taste – delicious.

Organic foods are nutritionally better for you, give you more energy, help you live longer and preserve youth. They are great for your skin, improve libido, regenerate cells, are free of toxins, are 100 per cent natural and keep New Zealand green and clean.

A BRIEF HISTORY IN TIME

For as long as we have been tending the earth, the only fertilisers available have been organic ones such as animal dung or compost – at least that was the case until 150 years ago. In the mid-1800s, chemists began to analyse the composition of plants and to produce inorganic – or chemical – fertilisers.

The harvests yielded from fertiliser applications were, at first, spectacular. However, the results began to wear off as the texture of the soil began to change to a dust-like consistency incapable of retaining moisture. Crop yields fell dramatically, while the incidence of pests and diseases rose sharply. This in turn led to the development of chemical pesticides, which were extremely poisonous – not just to the harmful insects, fungi and weeds they were intended for, but to the humans handling or consuming them.

As humans we have a choice as to how we farm our food and feed our bodies. It is our choices in the food we grow, and in the food we purchase and consume that will lead us to a healthier or unhealthier body and world. As is often said, we are what we eat.

GENETIC MODIFICATION

Genetically modified (GM) food is already present in our daily diet as a result of the steady importation of GM goods into New Zealand. It is estimated that there could be up to 500 processed foods containing up to 56 different GM ingredients already on sale. To date there have been 238 field trials of GM crops and animals in this country. These include GM crops of potato, barley, sugar-beet, broccoli, maize and salmon.

Genetic modification is an artificial manipulation of the natural genes within the chemistry of the living cell. Basically, a gene from one plant or animal is mixed with a gene from another plant or animal to create a new specimen or life-form that can grow faster or be resistant to certain chemical sprays.

For example, to date, a gene from a fish has been crossed with a tomato gene to create a winter-growing tomato; human genes have been crossed with cow genes to create a milk product more like human milk; Round Up-resistant crops have been engineered to enable farmers to spray fields with Round Up chemicals, which kill bugs and weeds without destroying crops.

The rapid introduction of GM food is alarming. Some 20 million hectares of transgenic (cross-species) crops were planted in the USA in 1998 along with another 2.8 million hectares in Canada. Around 40 genetically modified farm plants including corn, potato and tomato have so far been developed.

While I acknowledge that GM foods may be a fantastic breakthrough for science, I have a number of concerns: primarily that we have no idea what the future outcome of eating these foods will be. To alter the DNA or gene of a plant or animal in this way is cross-breeding species, which would never normally happen in a million years of evolution.

GM foods do not feel right to me. They do not feel safe for my child. They do not feel balanced. I do not like them at all.

Genetically modified foods can never be part of the organic farming philosophy or practice.

USING THIS BOOK

The four-level process is easy to use and gives quick results. I've created recipes that are extremely easy to follow and are designed to give balance.

The book is divided into sections of **energising**, **cleansing**, **strengthening** and **toning** foods. For complete balance, simply ensure that your plate includes a food choice from each of these sections.

Remember to regularly include simple grain and salad dishes without flavouring: only two or three dishes on each plate need the flavouring described through the book. For example, your plate should look similar to the one illustrated on page 13.

You'll notice that **energising** foods are predominantly the pressed salads and miso soups; the **cleansing** foods are salads, seaweeds and vegetables dishes; the **strengthening** foods are beans and proteins; the **toning** foods are grains. While I recommend the four-level process for balance, please don't become obsessive about this. Just 60 per cent of your diet eaten in this manner is enough to make a tremendous difference to your health, fitness and energy levels.

EXAMPLE OF A FOUR-LEVEL MEAL – CLOCKWISE FROM LEFT: RICE AND AMARANTH BALLS (P. 86); EXOTIC TONIC GREENS (P. 38); AZUKI BEANS WITH KOMBU AND PUMPKIN (P. 68); PRESSED RADISH AND COURGETTE WITH WAKAME (P. 32)   ◗ ◗ ◗

Try eating this way for dinner or lunch. I've included separate sections on breakfasts, soups, desserts, stir-fries and one-pot meals designed for variety, simplicity and for creating balance.

Every recipe has interesting information about how the food affects your body, or points of historical interest.

A FUTURE VISION

The time has come to inspire a new growth of quality pure organic foods.

Our organic farmers are serious people who put a lot of time and effort into the stringent checks and procedures needed to ensure that their produce is totally pure.

Growing food in this natural, ecologically sustainable way is, I believe, the future direction this country should take. It makes common sense, both in terms of our health and our economic wellbeing.

New Zealand is particularly suited to gaining a global niche as supreme organic producers. We are isolated from the rest of the world's pollution, we have a strong organic composition in our soils, and the potential exists to create a huge export market.

We are a small country that makes a point of being first. Organic farming is our challenge and to be 100 per cent organic is possible. Most farmers I speak to are keen to embrace organics as a commercially viable operation. The numbers stack up. I can see the possibility of creating an organic nation where farmers work together to share knowledge and resources.

Eating organics is a big part of my vision for people to re-embrace health in a way that will transform their lives to a better quality of being. I believe we have the energy, knowledge and ability to take on this challenge. We have a beautiful country with a great future.

NEW TASTES AND TEXTURES

The recipes I've included in this book will introduce you to a new language of foods — foods that have a powerful effect on body balance. These foods include many different grains, sea vegetables and seasonings that offer high-quality organic nutrition and a fantastic taste. They offer a wonderful array of new tastes and textures.

Every food has an effect on body balance and it's your choice in food that makes the difference.

AMARANTH
A small grain that ranges in colour from yellow through to purple. It is high in protein, fibre and essential amino acids and has a strengthening, toning action on the body. This grain was well known to the Aztecs. An excellent grain for toning the abdomen.

APPLE CIDER VINEGAR
Apple cider vinegar is made from fermented apples to bring out essential enzymes that help remove accumulated toxins in the intestinal tract.

ARAME

Arame is a brown seaweed with a mild taste. Seaweeds can be used in a wide variety of recipes and need to be washed before use. They are a wonderful food for the digestive system and actually help eliminate toxins from the body. Arame is high in fibre, carbohydrates, niacin, iron, calcium and iodine. It helps lower the blood pressure and provides resilience to the cell.

AZUKI BEANS

Enliven muscle tone. Azuki beans are a powerful protein for building up tired kidneys and giving a more refined muscle tone.

BALSAMIC VINEGAR

Balsamic vinegar is made from organically grown grapes and fermented to bring out essential enzymes. This vinegar is a great balance for meat eaters and a powerful detoxifier.

BANCHA TEAS

BANCHA TWIG TEA

Also known as kukicha, this smooth beverage is made from the twigs and stems of tea bushes. The tea is picked when there is no tannin in the plant and therefore contains no caffeine. This tea is very alkalising and has calming qualities. It is an excellent tea to take for stomach or menstrual cramps, and an ideal tea to strengthen the body after illness, fatigue or childbirth. Drink two to three cups a day.

BANCHA TEA WITH TAMARI

A blood tonic tea that is especially good to help recovery from colds, flu and general fatigue. It can also be used to stimulate erections in males. To be effective you need to take one cup daily over several weeks. Add half a cup of tamari per cup of bancha to savour its potent effects.

BARLEY

This rich and nourishing grain, high in the B vitamins, fibre and protein has been eaten by humans for millennia. Barley that has been lightly rubbed to remove the husk is known as pot barley and has the most bran and nutrients. Pearl barley, which has been polished, is easy to digest and has healing properties for the liver.

BROWN RICE VINEGAR

A naturally brewed and fermented vinegar made from brown rice. Aged in wooden kegs over a year-long process, the vinegar has a deep dark colour with a hearty, rounded flavour. It is rich in amino acids, stimulating to the digestive system, and helps break down and disperse fat. Use to add extra flavour and goodness to salad dressings, stir-fries, sauces, spreads and dips.

BUCKWHEAT

A small triangular grain that comes from a herbaceous plant belonging to the rhubarb family. Buckwheat is rich in iron, calcium, niacin and protein. The grain has a heat-generating ability, which makes it a very strengthening food, especially good for the lungs, bladder and kidneys. Often people who are allergic to grain gluten can tolerate buckwheat well. Buckwheat is the most effective fluid-absorbing grain and is therefore excellent for expelling fluid from the legs or abdomen.

CHICKPEAS

Chickpeas are the most effective fluid-absorbing protein. They are great for extracting fluid from the thighs, bottom and abdomen. Ideal for people who retain fluid.

DAIKON

A long white radish with a sharp taste when raw, which mellows with cooking. It has a strong healing modality on the body, which includes dissolving excess fat and mucus, and is excellent for weight loss. Daikon reduces fever when made into a tea and relieves the itchiness of bites and rashes when applied externally. Daikon can be added to soups and stir-fries, and can be steamed or baked. It is the most powerful fat dissolver.

DAIKON DRINKS

These are healing drinks that can reduce fevers, work as a diuretic and help dissolve fat and mucus.

To reduce fever: Mix half a cup of freshly grated daikon with a teaspoon of tamari and a quarter teaspoon of freshly grated ginger. Pour hot water over mixture and drink hot.

To work as a diuretic: Take two tablespoons of daikon juice and add a pinch of sea salt, six tablespoons of water, and boil. Take the drink once a day, but never for more than three consecutive days.

To dissolve fat and mucus: Mix one tablespoon of freshly grated daikon and 10 drops of tamari, pour hot water over mixture and drink. Take just before sleeping, but not for more than seven consecutive days.

ECHINACEA TEA

The echinacea herb dramatically increases the production of white blood cells in the body, which helps eliminate infectious disease. The tea helps strengthen the immune system and is ideal to take when run down or fighting a cold.

EXOTIC TONIC GREENS

A large leaf salad mix combination of salad greens — pungent, sour, bitter, sweet, cleansing and mineral greens.

GAMASIO

(See 'Sesame seaweed shake', p. 19.)

GREEN TEA

Helps dissolve and rid the body of animal fats and excess cholesterol. Take one cup per day. Green tea is not recommended for people who are ill.

HIJIKI

A thick, dark sea vegetable with a strong taste, hijiki is rich in iron, protein and vitamins. It has a healing action for the blood, intestines and hair.

KARENGO

A New Zealand purple/green-coloured sea vegetable that is rich in carbohydrates, protein and vitamins. Karengo and other seaweeds contribute to good skin and shiny hair.

CLOCKWISE FROM LEFT: CHICKPEAS, AZUKI BEANS, QUINOA, BLACK LENTILS, WHITE RICE, BARLEY, MILLET ▶ ▶ ▶

KOMBU

Kombu is a brown kelp that has a dense leathery texture and needs to be cooked well to soften it up. It is rich in vitamins, iodine and calcium and makes a high-mineral blood tonic. When added to beans during the cooking process it reduces the cooking time, makes them more digestible and reduces flatulence.

KOMBU TEA

Helps purify the blood and remineralise the body. Place a strip of kombu in three cups of water and bring to the boil. Reduce heat and simmer for 10 minutes. Remove the kombu before serving.

LENTILS

Lentils break down fat. These small, disk-shaped beans have a distinctive flavour and a rather firm texture. They increase sluggish metabolism, help with constipation and assist the body to break down fat.

MAPLE SYRUP

A quick-releasing sugar fuel that goes well with breakfasts or desserts. The natural sweeteners I use in my recipes – maple syrup and brown rice malt – all come from good organic sources.

MILLET

A small, round, yellow-coloured cereal grain that is high in protein and easy for the body to digest. Millet contains iron, niacin and essential amino acids and is a body-balancing alkaline grain. It is a healing food, especially for the digestive system, spleen and pancreas, and is one of the most alkalising of all the grains.

MISO

Miso is considered to be an anti-cancer food. It is a fermented grain or bean made into a paste during a fermentation process which can take up to three years. Miso is rich in amino acids, enzymes, carbohydrates, vitamins and minerals. It aids digestion, alkalises the blood and helps build strong intestines by renewing intestinal flora. Miso is a highly detoxifying food and also helps clear nicotine and radioactive substances from the body. There are several types of miso available including the dark miso made from soya beans and barley and the light or mugi miso made from brown rice, which has a sweeter, lighter taste. Add a teaspoon to your favourite vegetable soup or stew for instant super nutrition.

NOODLES

Noodles – especially udon and soba noodles – form an important part of organic balanced eating. Hearty udon noodles are made from wholewheat flour; soba noodles from buckwheat flour. These noodles are considered to carry the life force because they have been kneaded, rolled and cut, as opposed to traditional noodles which are made with fine flour and commercial machinery.

NORI

The sushi seaweed, nori has to be toasted before use. Nori is a sea vegetable rich in iron, protein, calcium and vitamins and has been cultivated by the Japanese for 300 years. It is often used for wrapping rice balls and sushi or can be cut into strips and used as a garnish for soups. It has a healing action in reducing cholesterol levels.

OATS

This is an exercise grain. Oats contain the highest amount of oil and provide an excellent fuel for physically active people.

Oats are warming and strengthening, they help lower cholesterol, and are great for the skin. Rolled oats have been steamed, then rolled; whole oats have had their outer husk removed; scotch oats have been steamed, then cut.

OILS
Organic oils include cold-pressed sesame, corn, sunflower, olive and flax. These oils are free of artificial chemicals and preservatives, full of flavour and give the body balance. They are created without destroying the delicate chemical composition of oils, which can cause rancidity. Throughout this book I have used different oils for different recipes as each oil carries specific qualities: sesame and sunflower oils are ideal for quick sautés; corn oil is ideal for long sautés as it creates a richer end-product; flaxseed and olive oils should be eaten unheated because of their delicate qualities.

PICKLED GINGER
Ginger that has been pickled in a mixture containing rice malt. It is the most powerful condiment for healing the liver.

PINTO BEANS
An energy fuel. Pinto beans are great for athletes as this small oval bean is a fantastic source of carbohydrates.

QUINOA
A tiny yellow grain, quinoa is the gold of all the grains. It is the highest-protein grain and creates a strong, sinuous muscle, the ideal food for people who want to look toned. Quinoa is also a powerful healing grain that should be eaten daily when recovering from serious illnesses such as cancer. It is rich in amino acids, iron, calcium, phosphorus, the B vitamins and fat. A food well known to the Incas.

RICE MALT
Rice malt is a delicate sweetener made from sprouted brown rice and barley by a traditional Japanese method. It is a slow-releasing sweetener that offers a prolonged source of energy and a subtle taste.

RICE MILK
A light fresh milk that is low in fat and is very easy to digest. Rice milk soothes the digestive organs.

RICE: SHORT GRAIN BROWN
A great carbohydrate food that provides fuel for active people and also works to calm the nervous system. Short grain brown rice has powerful toning qualities and is ideal for swollen intestines and a bloated stomach. Short grain brown rice is the staple in my recipes due to its neutral qualities and because it cooks easily with all the other grains.

SALT
Organic salt is high in minerals and trace elements essential for building healthy bones and muscles. It stimulates the metabolism, cleanses the blood and provides the body with important trace elements necessary for body function.

SEED MUSTARD
Organically grown mustard seeds carry a light opening quality that increases metabolic action and helps the liver break down fats.

SESAME SEAWEED SHAKE (GAMASIO)
A shake made from dry-roasted sesame seeds, seaweeds and sea salt. It can be used as a sprinkle flavouring on any meal. Gamasio takes salt into the intestine, which alkalises and heals this region. It is ideal for abdominal tone and

stimulates the circulation. Gamasio has been used throughout Asia for centuries to heal the digestive organs. Have one teaspoon per day and feel the difference.

SHOYU

A high-quality soy sauce that has been brewed traditionally. I liken shoyu to a good-quality wine, high in enzymes and nutrients, as opposed to soy sauce, which is a more like a poor quality wine that has been mixed and popped into a bottle with no fermentation process. Shoyu is a delicious seasoning that goes well with grains or noodles. It has alkalising properties and strengthens the blood.

SOYA MILK

This creamy milk is delightful to add to breakfasts or desserts. It is ideal for people who don't wish to eat dairy products.

TAMARI

Tamari looks very similar to shoyu, the difference being that tamari is the liquid taken from the top of the miso fermentation process. Tamari has a richer, creamier flavour and is considered a stronger, more powerful seasoning than shoyu. It is ideal for people recovering from illness, who have been feeling weak, fatigued or suffering from low libido.

TEMPEH

Tempeh is a fermented soya bean cake. Its active ingredients enhance the enzymes necessary for good health. This protein is a power hit.

TOFU

Tofu is a fermented soya bean curd. Tofu has texture and absorbs flavour, which is essential for variety and balance. Organic tofu is made from GM-free soya beans.

UMEBOSHI VINEGAR

Umeboshi vinegar is perhaps the most powerful antioxidant. Umeboshi is made from pickled plums and is high in enzymes and minerals which have a rejuvenating effect on the body. Umeboshi products also help the liver to clean out artificial chemicals from the body. The umeboshi plums counteract stomach upsets, travel sickness and hangovers. Add a splash of umeboshi vinegar to salad greens or use in the high-enzyme pressed salads.

WAKAME

Wakame seaweed has antibacterial properties. An elegant seaweed with a delicate texture, it is very tender and should not be cooked for too long. It is ideal in soups, beans and vegetable salads, including pressed salads and sautés. It is high in calcium, iron, vitamin A and C, niacin and protein. My favourite seaweed.

WHEAT

Wheat is the most widely consumed food in the world. Because of its uplifting energy qualities, wheat is healing to the liver. Although many people suffer from allergies to this grain, it is my belief that the over-consumption of bread, and the yeast used in modern baking methods is more damaging than the pure wheat grain itself. It is also considered that many allergies arise from the chemicals used in modern wheat-farming methods – which is why organic wheat is essential.

NOODLES LEFT TO RIGHT: SOBA; CORN-QUINOA; UDON; WHOLE WHEAT; BUCKWHEAT-WHEAT BLEND; REFINED WHEAT ▶ ▶ ▶

CUTTING STYLES

Different cutting styles enhance the presentation and look of your food. The various cutting techniques that follow will beautify and add variety to your meals.

All great chefs recognise the difference a cutting technique can make to the flavour of your food. It enhances the texture, taste and overall energy of the final food dish.

1. DIAGONAL SLICING
Slice vegetables on the diagonal.

2. ROUNDS
Slice the vegetable straight across.

3. DICING
A technique for cutting round vegetables – for example, onions. Cut the vegetable in half lengthwise, then cut toward the root, thinly slicing as you go but leaving the root intact. Then cut the vegetable lengthwise. Finally, chop off the root.

4. HALF MOON (ROOT VEG)
Cut the vegetable in half lengthwise and then cut straight across.

5. IRREGULAR CUTS
A method of preparing vegetables for soups and stews. Cut diagonal slices, then turn the vegetable 180 degrees and make another diagonal cut in the same direction.

6. JULIENNE STRIPS
Slice vegetable lengthwise in half then lengthwise again into long strips.

7. QUARTER
Cut the vegetable in half lengthwise and then in half lengthwise again. Then cut the vegetable across.

8. MATCHSTICKS
First cut the vegetables on the diagonal, then pile them almost on top of each other and cut lengthwise into thin strips.

9. HALF MOON (ROUND VEG)
A method for cutting round vegetables – for example, turnips, onions and beets. Cut the vegetable in half then slice finely into the centre of the vegetable. Make the slices as thin or thick as desired.

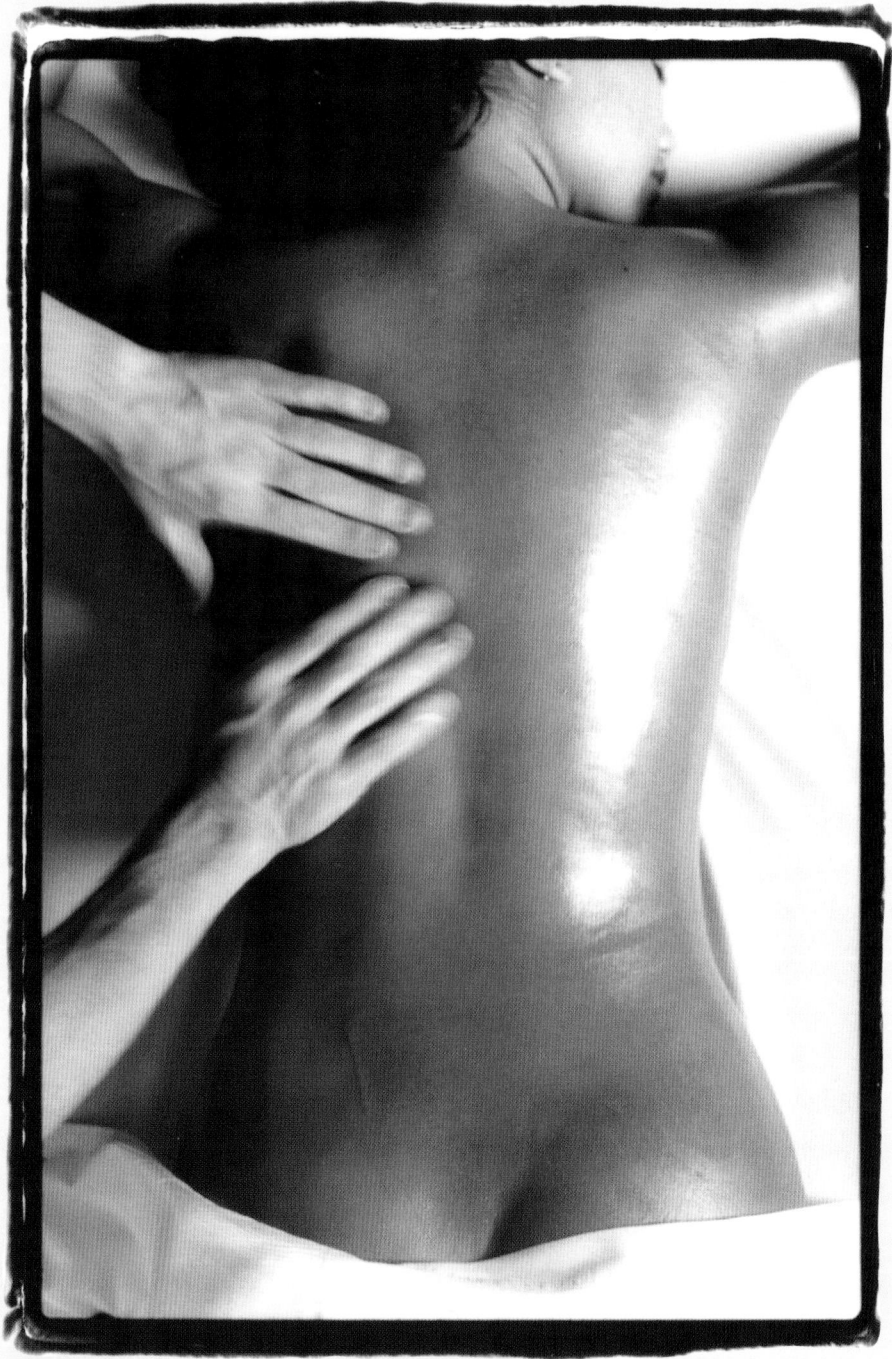

ENERGISING FOODS

The following recipes have been designed
to give you more energy and increase
metabolic activity. Pressed salads and
pickles are delicious and carry essential
enzymes that activate cell vitality through
a metamorphic process within the
digestive system.

ENERGISING

PRESSED SALADS

Pressed salads work to carry salt deep into the intestinal tract. The vegetable fibre passes quickly through the stomach and then slowly releases the alkalising salts into the intestine. The stomach therefore remains more acidic, allowing it to break down food, while the intestines become alkaline, which aids in the digestive process.

The enzymes within the pressed salad also help build intestinal flora, which provides elasticity of the intestines and helps build abdominal tone.

High-enzyme pressed salads are essential for improved digestion and metabolic activity, which increase body energy.

MAKING A PRESSED SALAD

There are fundamentally two ways of making a pressed salad, either by using a salad press or by hand.

Salad presses are available from Organic Home Delivery or from selected health food stores nationwide.

A pressed salad is essentially a pickling and fermentation process whereby firm pressure is applied on vegetables. This pressure can be applied by tightening down the salad press or by gently squeezing the vegetables by hand. Either method provides a similar effect: moisture is driven out of the vegetable while the seasoning salt — for example, umeboshi or shoyu — is pulled to the centre of the vegetable.

PRESSED RED ONION AND CUCUMBER SALAD ▶

A high-enzyme, blood-cleansing salad. Onions help break down fat by increasing metabolic activity.

1¹/₂ cups red onion, sliced
1¹/₂ cups cucumber, peeled and sliced into fine half rounds
1 teaspoon umeboshi vinegar

▶ Place all ingredients in a salad bowl and hand press for 2–3 minutes. Serve.

PRESSED CUCUMBER ▶

Cucumber is one of the earliest cultivated vegetables and is thought to have originated in India. It has cooling properties and is great for summer balance.

2 cups cucumber, sliced finely on a diagnoal
1 teaspoon brown rice vinegar
1 teaspoon umeboshi vinegar

▶ Mix cucumber and vinegars thoroughly in a salad press.
▶ Tighten pressure on press and let sit for 1–3 hours.
▶ Remove pickles from press and squeeze out excess liquid. Serve.

PRESSED SPRING ONION AND CARROT ▶

This quick pressed salad adds colour and flavour to your meal.

1 cup carrot, cut into diagonals
1 cup spring onions, cut into diagonals
¹/₂ teaspoon tamari

▶ Place all ingredients in salad bowl.
▶ Hand press for 1–2 minutes.

SPRING ONION AND WAKAME PRESSED SALAD ▶

Tender and mild, spring onions are easy to hand press.

¹/₂ cup wakame seaweed
2 cups spring onions, chopped finely
¹/₂ teaspoon umeboshi vinegar

▶ Wash and soak wakame seaweed for 5 minutes.
▶ Place spring onions in salad bowl with umeboshi vinegar. Hand press for 1 minute.
▶ Slice wakame seaweed finely and mix with pressed spring onions.

HAND PRESSING RED ONION AND CUCUMBER SALAD ▶ ▶ ▶

PRESSED CUCUMBER, CABBAGE AND WAKAME SALAD ▶

This salad is especially beneficial to the intestines. Cabbage is the most effective fluid-absorbing vegetable and tones the abdominal area.

1 cup cucumber, sliced very finely, on a diagonal
1 cup cabbage, finely shredded
1 teaspoon umeboshi vinegar
¹/₂ cup wakame seaweed

▶ Hand press or squeeze umeboshi vinegar into vegetables for 2–5 minutes.
▶ Soak wakame in water for 15–30 minutes and drain.
▶ Chop wakame and add to the salad.

COURGETTE AND CUCUMBER PRESSED SALAD ▶

Wakame is an elegant seaweed with a delicate texture. It has antibacterial properties and is delicious in pressed salads.

1 cup courgettes, chopped into thin half moons
1 cup cucumber, chopped into thin half moons
¹/₄ cup wakame seaweed, washed and cut finely
1 teaspoon brown rice vinegar

▶ Place all ingredients in salad press and press for 1–4 hours.

PRESSED CELERY AND COURGETTE SALAD ▶

The crisp fibre of celery makes this pressed salad a great intestinal cleanser, strong with umeboshi, to activate sluggish intestinal congestion that can lead to cancer.

1 cup celery, cut into 4 cm julienne strips
1 cup courgettes, sliced on a diagonal
2 teaspoons umeboshi vinegar

▶ Gently hand press celery and courgettes with umeboshi vinegar for 3 minutes. Serve.

PRESSED CELERY SALAD ▶

Celery was prized as both a food and medicine by the ancient Romans, Greeks and Egyptians. It is native to Italy with the modern variety developed in Italy in the 16th century.

1¹/₂ cups celery, sliced finely, on a diagonal
¹/₂ teaspoon umeboshi vinegar

▶ Hand press celery with umeboshi vinegar for 2–3 minutes. Serve.

CABBAGE PRESS ▶

Hand-pressed cabbage is tender and great for the digestion.

2 cups cabbage, finely shredded
¼ teaspoon sea salt
1 teaspoon brown rice vinegar
1 tablespoon lemon zest

▶ Place cabbage in a salad bowl with salt, brown rice vinegar and lemon zest.
▶ Gently hand press for 2–3 minutes. Serve.

PRESSED CHINESE CABBAGE ▶

Chinese cabbage is also known as celery cabbage or pe-tsai. It has been used in China and parts of Asia since the 5th century.

2 cups Chinese cabbage, cut into strips
¾ cup cucumber, cut into rounds
¾ cup celery, cut in diagonals
¾ cup daikon, sliced very thinly
1 teaspoon umeboshi vinegar

▶ Place prepared vegetables into a salad press with umeboshi vinegar.
▶ Leave to press for 45 minutes–1 hour

PRESSED RED CABBAGE AND RADISH ▶

Red cabbage is in season from spring until mid-summer and adds colour to any meal.

2 cups red cabbage, shredded
1 cup radish, cut into thin half moons
1 teaspoon umeboshi vinegar

▶ Press vegetables in a salad press with umeboshi vinegar for 1–3 hours.

CARROT PRESS ▶

So quick, so colourful and so delicious. An excellent source of Vitamin A which is good for the eyes, muscles, flesh and skin.

1½ cups carrots, sliced on a diagonal
½ teaspoon umeboshi vinegar

▶ Place carrots in a salad bowl with umeboshi vinegar.
▶ Gently hand press by squeezing the ingredients together with hands for 1–2 minutes. Serve.

CLOCKWISE FROM BOTTOM LEFT: TUNA STEAK (P. 78), SALAD GREENS, BROWN RICE (P. 82), CARROT PRESS ▶ ▶ ▶

PRESSED RADISH AND DAIKON ▶

This great pickle has both radishes working towards breaking down fat and removing toxins.

1 cup red radishes, sliced into half moons
1 cup daikon, sliced on a diagonal
1 teaspoon umeboshi vinegar

▶ Hand press vegetables with umeboshi vinegar for 1–2 minutes. Serve.

LETTUCE, RADISH AND CARROT PRESSED SALAD ▶

Lettuce was first cultivated in 15th-century England, though the vegetable was known to the Greeks and Romans, who used it as a medicine to aid sleep. There are many varieties of modern lettuce including cos, red and green coral, endive, buttercrunch and iceberg.

2 cups iceberg lettuce, finely sliced
½ cup radishes, finely sliced
½ cup carrots, chopped into half moons
½ teaspoon sea salt

▶ Mix vegetables together in a salad press with sea salt.
▶ Press firmly for 1–3 hours. Serve.

PRESSED RADISH AND COURGETTE WITH WAKAME ▶

Pickled radishes are great for cleansing the liver and helping metabolise fats.

½ cup wakame seaweed
1 cup red radishes, sliced into thin rounds
1 cup courgettes, sliced into thin rounds
1 teaspoon umeboshi vinegar

▶ Wash wakame seaweed and soak for 5 minutes then cut into 5 cm long pieces.
▶ Place radishes and courgettes into salad press with wakame seaweed.
▶ Add umeboshi vinegar to mixture. Place top on press and screw down tightly. Leave mixture to press for 1–3 hours. Serve.

LEFT, TOP TO BOTTOM: BOILED CUCUMBER AND BROCCOLI (P. 49); BARLEY SPRINKLED WITH GAMASIO (P. 82); PRESSED RADISH AND DAIKON. RIGHT: PINTO BEANS, TOFU AND CARROTS (P. 71) ▶ ▶ ▶

BROCCOLI PICKLES ▶

Broccoli is a member of the brassica family. It was first cultivated in Italy and has cancer prevention properties.

1 cup small broccoli florets
1 teaspoon lemon zest
1½ teaspoons sea salt
1½ cups water, purified or boiled and cooled

▶ In a jar, mix sea salt with water.
▶ Add broccoli and lemon zest. The mixture needs to be left uncovered for 2–3 days at room temperature while the pickling process takes place. Each day, push the florets down in the water with a chopstick or other utensil to remove fermented air.
▶ Try cauliflower in this way also. Drain and store in the fridge. Pickles keep for 3 days.

ONION PICKLES ▶

Onions have been around for 5000 years and are thought to have originated in Central Asia. Onions are master fat dissolvers and thin down the blood for easy weight loss and detoxification.

2 cups onions, cut into half moons
1½ cups water
½ cup tamari

▶ Place all ingredients in a jar.
▶ Leave mixture uncovered to pickle for 2–3 days at room temperature. As above, push down with chopstick to remove fermented air.
▶ Drain and store in the fridge. Keeps for 3 days.
▶ Carrots, cabbage or daikon can also be pickled using this recipe.

PRESSED DAIKON AND CUCUMBER PICKLES ▶

Pressed daikon has been used for hundreds of years in Asia to cleanse the intestines and restore liver function for proper digestion.

2 cups cucumber, scored with a fork and sliced into diagonals
1 cup daikon, scored with a fork and sliced into diagonals
1 teaspoon shoyu

▶ Place ingredients into salad press with umeboshi vinegar.
▶ Screw down lid of press and leave mixture to pickle for 1–3 hours.

CLEANSING FOODS

The cleansing foods include salads,
seaweeds, vegetables and fruit.
Cleansing foods permeate deep into the
tissue and expel unwanted toxins.
These foods are high in minerals, vitamins
and oxygen – which have a rejuvenating
effect on the body.

CLEANSING

EXOTIC TONIC GREENS

'Exotic tonic greens' is the name I attribute to a large leaf salad mix. It is the most powerful food for cleansing the body and carries high levels of chlorophyll. Chlorophyll is the life-blood of the plant and has a rejuvenating effect on the body.

The chlorophyll greens carry oxygen, which removes toxins and revitalises body tissue.

The oxygen-carrying capacity of the blood created by high-chlorophyll greens makes it near impossible for bacteria or viruses such as colds, flu, thrush or candida to exist. This makes the greens extremely powerful blood cleansers.

Chlorophyll greens also contain iron, calcium and potassium, all essential for energy and vitality.

The combination of the various flavours offers energy dynamics within the cleansing process.

'Exotic tonic greens' can include any combination of the following salad greens — the different flavours of which induce different effects on the body.

Pungent greens stimulate the body's energy system to disperse and break down fat. Pungent greens include red mustard greens, daikon tops, rocket, mizuna and watercress.

Sour greens have an uplifting quality that opens up the body and organs. Sour flavours help the organs function correctly by increasing the circulation deep within the tissue. Sour greens include sorrel, red chard, basil and spinach.

Bitter greens have an astringent effect causing the contraction of body tissues, flushing out excess fluid and toning the abdominal area. Bitter greens include puha, chicory, frisee, radicchio and endive.

Sweet greens nurture and stabilise the body's energy systems as well as calming fragmented body imbalances that can cause cellulite. Sweet greens include kale, lettuce, mibuna, bok choy and tat soi.

SEAWEEDS

An easy and delicious way of introducing minerals to your body. Classically called seaweeds, they are actually sea vegetables that work to expel toxins and aid your body's own mineral equilibrium.

It is my firm belief that it is preferable to include seaweed in the diet to gain a good nutritional balance, rather than to take mineral or vitamin supplements.

RAW VEGETABLES

Throughout this section you will see many recipes using raw fresh vegetables, which are an essential part of the cleansing process.

COOKED VEGETABLES

Boiled or long sautéd vegetables hydrate the body tissue, which helps eliminate toxins. I know many people concern themselves with nutrient loss from cooking — this is a reality, but the balance of raw vegetables, seasonal grains, beans and pressed salads within the four levels of eating allows you to enjoy cooked vegetables without a concern about mineral loss. The hydration of body tissue is a rejuvenating experience.

FRUIT

Fruit are great cleansing foods which work rapidly at detoxifying the body. They help eliminate breads, meats, sausages, hamburgers and chemically-laden food.

The powerful cleansing properties of fruit make them an ideal summer detoxifier, but you need to be aware that in winter, excess fruit can chill the body.

Fresh seasonal fruit are a great source of vitamins, taste delicious and are an essential part of the diet. However, a diet too high in fruit can be so cleansing that it can fatigue the body unless the fructose sugars are burnt out daily with exercise.

An excessive fruit diet can lead to fluid retention, cellulite, puffiness in the face, abdominal swelling and atrophied muscle tissue.

If you are a man suffering from low libido, I recommend cutting your fruit intake to three pieces per week. Remember that consuming fruit juice is the same as eating fruit.

MESCLUN SALAD MIX WITH CARROT AND DAIKON ◗

A mesclun salad mix is tender with young leaves similar to the exotic tonic greens. They are not as strong to taste, but still have powerful cleansing effects on the body.

1¹/₂ cups mesclun salad mix
¹/₂ cup carrots, cut into half moons
¹/₂ cup daikon, cut into julienne strips
1 lemon

◗ Mix vegetables together with salad mix and lemon juice. Serve.

SUMMER SALAD ◗

A light refreshing summer salad.

120 grams exotic tonic greens
¹/₂ cup courgettes, diagonally cut
1 cup spring onions, cut into ovals
1 teaspoon lemon juice
1 teaspoon olive oil
1 teaspoon water
1 teaspoon shoyu

◗ Place exotic tonic greens in a salad bowl with courgettes and spring onions.
◗ Squeeze lemon juice into a cup with olive oil, water and shoyu. Mix these ingredients thoroughly.
◗ Pour dressing over salad. Serve.

EXOTIC SALAD ◗

A light and cleansing salad.

120 grams exotic tonic greens
1 cup mung bean sprouts
¹/₂ cup watercress
1 avocado
1 teaspoon white miso
1 tablespoon water
1 tablespoon lemon juice
1 tablespoon sesame seeds

◗ Place exotic tonic greens, mung bean sprouts, watercress and avocado slices in a salad bowl.
◗ Mix miso with water and a squeeze of lemon juice then pour dressing over salad. Sprinkle sesame seeds on top. Serve.
◗ Wash sesame seeds then roast in heavy-based frying pan for about 3-5 mins or until golden.

LEFT TO RIGHT, TOP TO BOTTOM: BLACK BEANS WITH CORN (P. 66); MESCLUN SALAD MIX WITH CARROT AND DAIKON; SPRING ONION AND WAKAME PRESSED SALAD (P. 26); SUSHI (P. 90) ◗ ◗ ◗

EXOTIC SALAD WITH TOMATOES ▶

Tomatoes originated from South America and first arrived in Europe in the 17th century. The fruit was initially considered dangerous as it is related to the Solanaceae family of poisonous plants, which includes deadly nightshade. Also in this family are potatoes, eggplants, tobacco and peppers. Tomatoes were known as 'pommes d'amour' or 'apples of love' by the French.

2 tomatoes, cut into quarters
1 avocado, cut into thick slices
120 grams exotic tonic greens
¼ cup parsley, finely cut
1 tablespoon brown rice vinegar
1 teaspoon olive oil
1 teaspoon shoyu
1 tablespoon sesame seaweed shake (Gomasio)

▶ Mix tomatoes and avocado in a salad bowl with exotic tonic greens and parsley.

▶ Mix brown rice vinegar, olive oil and shoyu then fold into salad. Sprinkle sesame seaweed shake on top of the salad. Serve.

GREEN SALAD WITH FLAXSEED OIL ▶

Flaxseed oil offers essential fatty acids from the omega group, which are easily transferred into body energy.

1 teaspoon flaxseed oil
1 teaspoon shoyu
1 teaspoon brown rice vinegar
120 grams mesclun salad mix

▶ Mix flaxseed oil, shoyu and brown rice vinegar to make dressing.

▶ Place greens into a bowl, add dressing and serve.

BLANCHED RADISHES ▶

Radishes are a very old vegetable, thought to be native to Asia or Egypt. The name comes from a Latin word meaning an easy-growing root. Radishes cooked in this way are gentle cleansers and can be eaten often throughout the summer months.

1 cup radishes, cut into quarters
1 teaspoon umeboshi vinegar

▶ Blanch or quickly boil radishes for 1 minute.

▶ Place cooked radishes in a salad bowl and splash with umeboshi vinegar – this keeps the colour of the radishes and tastes great.

WILD SALAD ▶

Rocket is native to the Mediterranean region and is related to the cresses. Rocket's hot, peppery flavour makes it especially cleansing and good for the liver.

1 cup rocket greens
¹/₂ cup watercress
1 cup lettuce, chopped
¹/₂ cup spring onions, chopped
¹/₂ cup cucumber, chopped
¹/₂ cup celery, chopped
¹/₄ cup parsley
1 teaspoon seed mustard
1 teaspoon flaxseed oil
1 teaspoon shoyu
1 teaspoon lemon juice
1 teaspoon water

▶ Place leafy greens in a salad bowl with all other vegetables chopped chunky or finely to suit your mood.
▶ Mix seed mustard, flaxseed oil, shoyu, lemon juice and water together and then fold into salad. Serve.

APPLE, ONION AND CUCUMBER SALAD ▶

Apples are one of the most widely grown fruits with over 3000 varieties in cultivation. Organic apples are becoming a huge export earner for New Zealand.

1 cup apples, diced
¹/₂ cup onions, diced
1 cup cucumber, finely sliced
1 tablespoon lemon juice
pinch sea salt

▶ Mix the apple, onion and cucumber together with a squeeze of lemon juice and a pinch of salt. Serve.

BEETROOT AND CARROT GRATE ▶

Beetroot has cleansing properties and grated raw is good for getting rid of worms in the intestines or, better still, preventing the occurrence.

¹/₂ cup beetroot, finely grated
¹/₂ cup carrots, coarsely grated
1 teaspoon brown rice vinegar

▶ Splash vegetables with brown rice vinegar. Serve.

GRATED CARROT AND APPLE ▶

Carrots originate from Afghanistan and were later introduced to Britain from Holland. This condiment is a delicious liver cleanser and a great antidote to constipation.

1 cup apples, coarsely grated
juice of 1 lemon
pinch sea salt
1 cup carrots, finely grated

▶ Squeeze lemon juice over apple to stop it going brown. Add a pinch of organic salt for mineral balance.
▶ Mix carrot with apple.
▶ Serve as a side dish or condiment to your meal.

GRATED DAIKON ▶

Daikon has powerful fat-dissolving properties and aids weight loss. It is beneficial for lung congestion, asthma and intestinal detoxification. This condiment is very good for balancing meat or cheese dishes.

³/₄ cup daikon, grated
1 fresh sprig parsley
1 teaspoon tamari

▶ Place daikon on a plate.
▶ Sprinkle centre of mixture with tamari and garnish with parsley.

GRATED DAIKON AND CARROT ▶

This daikon and carrot condiment is a cleansing experience – it is especially good for unpleasant body scent, mucus, pimples and kidney disorders.

¹/₂ cup carrots, finely grated
¹/₂ cup daikon, coarsely grated
1 teaspoon umeboshi vinegar

▶ Splash carrot and daikon with umeboshi vinegar and eat raw.

BEETROOT WITH UMEBOSHI VINEGAR ▶

Beetroot was known to the Greeks and Romans, who enjoyed eating the vegetable leaves. Beetroot are understood to have been under cultivation in the Middle East some 2000 years ago.

2 cups beetroot
1 tablespoon brown rice vinegar
1 tablespoon umeboshi vinegar

▶ To cook beetroot, bring pot of water to boil, wash beetroot and boil until soft – around half an hour depending on size.
▶ Remove beetroot from pot and allow to cool. Rub with hands to remove skin. Slice and place in a salad bowl.
▶ Add brown rice and umeboshi vinegars to bring out rich red flavour.

AVOCADO DIP ▶

Avocados originate from South America and gain their name from the Aztec name 'ahuacet'. There are over 500 varieties of avocado. This dip is ideal with crackers, celery or carrot sticks.

2 cups soft avocado, cut finely
1 cup tomatoes, diced
1 teaspoon sesame seaweed shake
1 teaspoon shoyu
1 teaspoon brown rice vinegar

▶ Place avocado and tomato in a bowl.
▶ Season mixture with sesame seaweed shake, and add shoyu and brown rice vinegar.
▶ Mix together with a fork. Serve.

BOILED BROCCOLI WITH BROWN RICE VINEGAR ▶

Pure organic brown rice vinegar has been fermented for two years and contains essential enzymes that build strong intestines.

1 cup broccoli florets, chopped
1 tablespoon brown rice vinegar

▶ Boil broccoli for 3 minutes. Drain.
▶ Place vegetables in a salad bowl with brown rice vinegar. Serve.

WATERCRESS SALAD ▶

The peppery flavour of watercress makes it a great blood purifier and fat dissolver. It also helps provide a good source of calcium, fibre and vitamins A and C.

1 cup carrots, cut into matchsticks
3 cups watercress
1 teaspoon brown rice vinegar

▶ Boil carrots for 1 minute. Place in bowl.
▶ In the same boiling water cook watercress for 1 minute, stirring mixture to ensure even cooking. Remove watercress, rinse in cold water and drain.
▶ Slice watercress and mix with carrots. Cover with brown rice vinegar. Serve.

CLOCKWISE FROM LEFT: MILLET WITH BROWN RICE VINEGAR (P. 92); PRESSED RED ONION AND CUCUMBER SALAD (P. 26); PINTO BEANS, TOFU AND CARROTS (P. 71); BOILED BROCCOLI WITH BROWN RICE VINEGAR ▶ ▶ ▶

KUMARA AND BROCCOLI SALAD ▶

Kumara is a great fuel food, combined with sesame seaweed shake, it is especially good for the digestive process.

2 cups kumara, cut into chips
1 cup broccoli, small florets
1 teaspoon olive oil
1 teaspoon apple cider vinegar
1 teaspoon sesame seaweed shake

▶ Boil kumara for 3 minutes and broccoli for approximately 2 minutes. Drain.
▶ Place the cooked vegetables in a salad bowl. Add olive oil, apple cider vinegar and sesame seaweed shake. Serve hot or cold.

ASPARAGUS AND BROCCOLI SALAD ▶

Asparagus originated in the Mediterranean and Asia. The vegetable was popular with ancient Greeks and Romans, who used it as a medicine. Asparagus is part of the immature shoot of tuberous lily roots.

1 bunch asparagus
1 cup broccoli, small florets
1 tablespoon brown rice vinegar

▶ Boil asparagus and broccoli for 3 minutes.
▶ Remove from water and place on a plate with brown rice vinegar. Serve hot or cold.

CUCUMBER AND GREEN BEAN SALAD ▶

Apple cider vinegar is great for purifying the intestines, especially for people who have eaten a lot of bread and meat.

$1/2$ cup wakame seaweed
1 cup green beans
2 cups cucumber, peeled and diced
1 teaspoon apple cider vinegar

▶ Wash wakame seaweed and soak for 10 minutes. Drain and cut finely.
▶ Blanch green beans and place in serving bowl with cucumber and wakame. Flavour with apple cider vinegar.

CARROT, GREEN BEAN AND COURGETTE BLANCHED SALAD ▶

A juicy hydrating summer salad.

$1/2$ cup carrots, chopped into quarters
1 cup courgettes, chopped into rounds
1 cup green beans
1 teaspoon apple cider vinegar

▶ Boil carrots for 2 minutes, add beans and courgettes and boil for another minute.
▶ Remove vegetables and immediately rinse with cold water to keep juicy and stop over-cooking.
▶ Flavour with apple cider vinegar.

CAULIFLOWER AND GREEN BEANS ▶

There are many varieties of fresh beans – butter, runner, French, broad, green – most of them originating in Central and South America. Broad beans are known as fava beans in Italy; French beans were brought to Europe from South and Central America in the 16th century.

1 cup cauliflower, large florets
1 cup green beans
1 teaspoon umeboshi vinegar

▶ Boil cauliflower for 5 minutes and beans for 2 minutes and place in a salad bowl.
▶ Add umeboshi vinegar. Serve.

BROCCOLI AND KUMARA TRIANGLES ▶

Maori brought kumara or sweet potato to New Zealand from Hawaiiki. The sweet potato was grown in Europe during the 16th and 17th centuries.

1 cup broccoli, small florets
2 cups kumara, cut into small chunky triangles
1 teaspoon flaxseed oil

▶ Cook kumara in boiling water for 3 minutes then add broccoli for a further minute.
▶ Place in a serving bowl with flaxseed oil. Serve hot.

BOILED CUCUMBER AND BROCCOLI ▶

Cucumber is really juicy when cooked for a few minutes. It provides a hydrating effect on the body and is a great dish for summer as it is very thirst-quenching.

1 cup cucumber, cut into 1 cm slices
1 cup broccoli, small florets
1 teaspoon brown rice vinegar

▶ Boil cucumber and broccoli for 2 minutes then place in a bowl with a splash of brown rice vinegar. Serve.

BOILED KALE ▶

Kale, also known as curly kale or collard greens, is a cabbage without a solid head. The vegetable originates from Asia and the Mediterranean. Kale is a very good green for building immune strength and rejuvenating a tired body.

3 cups kale
1 teaspoon brown rice vinegar

▶ Bring pot of water to boil ensuring there is enough to completely cover the kale.
▶ Place kale in pot and boil for 5 minutes.
▶ Remove kale and let cool.
▶ Roll kale tightly and chop finely on a diagonal. Place in a bowl and season with brown rice vinegar. Serve.

BOILED RED MUSTARD GREENS ▶

Mature red mustard greens grow as large as silverbeet and taste really hot. They are fantastic fat burners and help lower blood pressure. Boiling the greens takes away the seriously hot flavours and makes a delicious juicy green, which can be eaten often.

3 cups red mustard greens, sliced

▶ Boil red mustard greens for 2 minutes, drain and serve.

SILVERBEET, DAIKON AND CARROT BOILED SALAD ▶

Silverbeet was first regarded as a food by the Greeks and was also valued by the Romans. Silverbeet is also known as seakale beet, chard and Swiss chard. This is a balancing recipe for meat eaters as both the silverbeet and daikon help digest fats and meat.

3 cups silverbeet, cut into diagonal strips
1/2 cup daikon, cut into matchsticks
1/2 cup carrots, cut into matchsticks
1 teaspoon flaxseed oil
1 teaspoon umeboshi vinegar

▶ Boil all vegetables together for 2 minutes. Drain and place in a bowl.
▶ Mix vegetables thoroughly with flaxseed oil and umeboshi vinegar. Serve.

CAULIFLOWER AND SWEETCORN BOILED SALAD ▶

Sweetcorn has been grown for over 5000 years. It is native to Central America and arrived in Europe in the 16th century. A popular Maori dish is kangapiro – a dessert made from fermented sweetcorn.

1 1/2 cups cauliflower florets, chopped
4 sweetcorn cobs, chopped into 2 cm slices
1 tablespoon umeboshi vinegar

▶ Bring pot of water to boil and cook both corn and cauliflower for 2 minutes.
▶ Remove from water and place in a bowl. Season with umeboshi vinegar. Serve.

KUMARA, CAULIFLOWER AND BROCCOLI BOILED SALAD ▶

Both broccoli and cauliflower are members of the brassica family which contain certain qualities that inhibit the development of some cancers. Lemon juice helps the liver function properly and helps with the digestion of these vegetables.

1 cup kumara, chopped into 2 cm cubes
1 cup cauliflower florets, chopped
1 cup broccoli florets, chopped
1 tablespoon lemon juice
1 teaspoon sesame seaweed shake

▶ Place kumara in pot of boiling water and cook for 3 mintues, before adding cauliflower and broccoli. Boil for a further 2 minutes then drain and rinse in cold water.
▶ Place vegetables in a bowl and add lemon juice and sesame seaweed shake. Serve.

WATERCRESS AND WAKAME SALAD ▶

Watercress grows wild in streams and ditches and only recently has been cultivated with organic farming methods. It is related to the American cress and European winter cress.

1 cup wakame seaweed
2 cups watercress
1 teaspoon seed mustard

▶ Wash wakame seaweed and soak for 3 minutes, cut into bite-sized pieces then steam with watercress for 3 minutes.
▶ Place mixture in serving bowl and mix with seed mustard. Serve.

LETTUCE AND WAKAME SALAD ▶

Wakame cooks more quickly than other seaweeds. It turns a lovely translucent green and its thin outer fronds are delicate on the palate.

½ cup wakame seaweed
1 cup cucumber, sliced into thin rounds
1 cup iceberg lettuce, coarsely chopped

▶ Soak wakame for 3 minutes and then boil for 3 minutes. Rinse under cold water, drain and slice into 3 cm pieces.
▶ Mix all ingredients together and serve in a salad bowl.

CUCUMBER AND WAKAME SALAD ▶

A high-mineral salad.

¾ cup wakame seaweed
2 cups cucumber, finely sliced
1 teaspoon brown rice vinegar

▶ Wash wakame and soak in water for 10–15 minutes. Drain.
▶ Cut soaked wakame leaves into 2 cm pieces and place in salad bowl.
▶ Add cucumber to wakame with brown rice vinegar.

WAKAME AND GINGER ▶

Wakame and ginger help balance out organ tightness caused by eating too much bread, meat and salt.

2 cups wakame seaweed
¼ cup grated ginger
1 teaspoon tamari

▶ Wash wakame seaweed. Place in a pot and cover with water. Bring to the boil, reduce heat to low and simmer for 10 minutes.
▶ Remove wakame seaweed, drain and rinse with cold water then cut finely.
▶ Squeeze the grated ginger juice on top and season with tamari. Serve.

WAKAME PUMPKIN ❱

Wakame seaweed has antibacterial properties and should not be cooked for too long.

1 cup wakame seaweed
1¹/₂ cups pumpkin, cut into 1 cm cubes
1 tablespoon shoyu

❱ Wash wakame seaweed then soak for 3 minutes. Drain and slice.
❱ Boil pumpkin and simmer for 5 minutes in pot with lid on.
❱ Add wakame seaweed to pot and simmer for a further 2 minutes.
❱ Drain and season with shoyu. Serve hot or cold.

PUMPKIN, DAIKON AND CARROT NISHIME ❱

Pumpkin is native to the Americas where Indians knew it as askootasquash. Pumpkin belongs to the same family as squash and marrow. Winter pumpkin varieties include butternut, buttercup, spaghetti, acorn and hubbard. Summer varieties include choko, marrows, courgettes and scallopini.

1 strip kombu seaweed
1¹/₂ cups butternut or buttercup pumpkin, cut into chunks
1 cup carrots, cut into irregular pieces
³/₄ cup daikon, cut into irregular pieces
1 teaspoon tamari

❱ Place kombu seaweed on the bottom of a pot with 1 cm of water.
❱ Layer pumpkin, carrot and daikon on top of kombu seaweed. Add tamari and simmer with lid on tight for 20 minutes. This is a Japanese style of steaming whereby the minerals from the kombu seaweed are absorbed into the vegetables using a minimal amount of water. Caution is needed not to burn the pot – add water if needed. Serve.

PUMPKIN, CARROT AND PARSNIP NISHIME ❱

A high-mineral style of cooking. Great for winter balance.

1 strip kombu seaweed
1¹/₂ cups pumpkin, peeled and cut into 2.5 cm chunks
1¹/₂ cups carrot, cut into ovals
1¹/₂ cups parsnip, cut into ovals
1 teaspoon shoyu

❱ Add kombu seaweed to 1cm of water and bring to the boil. Add pumpkin, carrots and parsnip, in that order.
❱ Add shoyu and simmer on a low heat for 20 minutes. Serve.

ARAME, CARROT AND AVOCADO SALAD ▶

Arame seaweed helps lower blood pressure and is a delicious ingredient in any salad. Arame is one of the milder-tasting seaweeds.

³/₄ cup carrots, sliced into thin ovals
¹/₄ cup arame seaweed
1 avocado, sliced
1 teaspoon miso paste
1 tablespoon lemon juice
1 tablespoon water

▶ Boil carrots with arame seaweed for 3 minutes.
▶ Remove boiled carrots and arame seaweed from water and arrange on a plate with slices of avocado.
▶ Mix miso with lemon juice and water and pour over salad. Serve.

SAUTÉED CABBAGE ▶

Rich and satisfying, this dish can be flavoured with mustard, garlic, herbs or spice. Try adding noodles or rice for a simple one-pot meal.

1 teaspoon sesame oil
2 cups cabbage, finely sliced
¹/₄ teaspoon sea salt
1 tablespoon grated ginger

▶ Heat frying pan with sesame oil.
▶ Sauté cabbage for 5 minutes.
▶ Sprinkle with sea salt and cover, continuing to cook for 2–3 minutes. Sprinkle with grated ginger and serve hot.

SAUTÉED CABBAGE WITH POTATOES AND PUMPKIN ▶

Potatoes are the most popular vegetable in the world and are thought to be native to the Andes region of South America.

1¹/₂ cups potatoes, cut into 5 cm pieces
1¹/₂ cups cabbage, finely sliced
1 teaspoon sesame oil
1 teaspoon curry powder
1 cup pumpkin, grated
¹/₄ teaspoon sea salt

▶ Heat sesame oil in wok or frying pan. Add curry powder and lightly roast to release aroma. Add pumpkin and stir-fry for 3 minutes.
▶ Add potatoes, cabbage and sea salt to ¹/₂ cup water and cook covered for 10 minutes. Serve.

HIJIKI SALAD ▶

Hijiki is black in colour and shaped like pine-needles. It grows off the coast of China and Japan and is one of the most powerful seaweeds for purifying the blood.

¹/₂ cup hijiki seaweed
1 cup cucumber, sliced on a diagonal
¹/₂ cup red radishes, cut into thick rounds
¹/₂ cup red onion, diced
1 cup iceberg lettuce
¹/₂ cup alfalfa sprouts
¹/₂ cup watercress
1 tablespoon balsamic vinegar

▶ Wash hijiki and boil for 15 minutes. Remove from water, drain and leave to cool then slice into 3 cm pieces.
▶ Place all the ingredients in a bowl so that colours are well balanced and sprinkle with balsamic vinegar. Serve.

HIJIKI AND BROCCOLI WATER SAUTÉ ▶

The richness and strength of hijiki is renowned for its ability to raise the libido level.

³/₄ cup of hijiki seaweed
¹/₂ cup courgettes, chopped into small cubes
2 cups broccoli florets
2 teaspoons hatho miso

▶ Soak hijiki seaweed for 1 hour.
▶ Simmer hijiki in a frying pan in a cup of water for 20 minutes with lid on.
▶ Remove lid and add vegetables and miso dissolved in hot water. Simmer for a further 3 minutes. Serve.

SPRING SAUTÉ ▶

Ginger is a natural blood thinner for people with blood clots, lung congestion and skin problems. Ginger is a great cleanser of toxins and helpful generally for breaking down fat in the body.

1 cup courgettes, cut into diagonal ovals
1 cup spring onions, cut into diagonal ovals
¹/₄ cup fresh ginger, sliced into matchsticks
¹/₂ cup washed karengo seaweed
1 teaspoon sesame oil
1 teaspoon brown rice vinegar

▶ Heat frying pan with sesame oil and sauté ginger for 3 minutes.
▶ Add courgettes and spring onions and sauté for a further 3 minutes.
▶ Add karengo seaweed and season with shoyu and brown rice vinegar. Serve.

CARROT AND ONION LONG SAUTÉ ▶

You can eat this dish hot or cold. Organic onions are generally easier to grow in the South Island where they are not subject to disease and viruses. Non-organic onions and carrots are the most heavily sprayed vegetables.

3 cups onions, sliced into half moons
1 cup carrots, cut into irregular chunks
1 tablespoon sesame oil
1 teaspoon tamari

▶ Sauté vegetables in sesame oil and tamari for 3 minutes, then add 1 cup of water.
▶ Cook on low heat with lid on for 30–50 minutes. Serve.

ONION AND PUMPKIN LONG SAUTÉ ▶

The combination of onions and pumpkin cooked this way is so sweet and is traditionally used to revitalise the immune system.

3 cups onions, chopped into half moons
2 cups pumpkin, peeled and chopped into chunks.
1 tablespoon corn oil
1 tablespoon shoyu

▶ Sauté onions in corn oil for 5 minutes or until transparent. Add pumpkin and 1 cup of water to prevent burning.
▶ Place lid on frying pan and cook on a low heat for 1 hour. Add shoyu and serve.

CARAMELISED ONIONS ▶

Onions are an ancient vegetable, understood to have been grown for at least 5000 years. They are thought to have originated from central Asia. Onions were worshipped by the ancient Egyptians and were used as currency during the Middle Ages. This is a rich, satisfying, sweet dish, delicious next to rice or on crackers or bread.

4 cups onions, peeled and sliced into half moons.
1 tablespoon sesame oil
1 teaspoon lemon zest
1 teaspoon shoyu

▶ Heat frying pan with sesame oil and sauté onion for 5 minutes or until transparent.
▶ Add grated lemon zest and a little water to prevent burning. Add shoyu. Place lid on and leave on a low heat for about 1 hour.

CLOCKWISE FROM TOP LEFT: FRIED TEMPEH (P. 76); MILLET WITH MUNG BEAN SPROUTS AND
CARROTS (P. 95); CUCUMBER AND WAKAME SALAD (P. 51); ONION AND PUMPKIN LONG SAUTÉ ▶ ▶ ▶

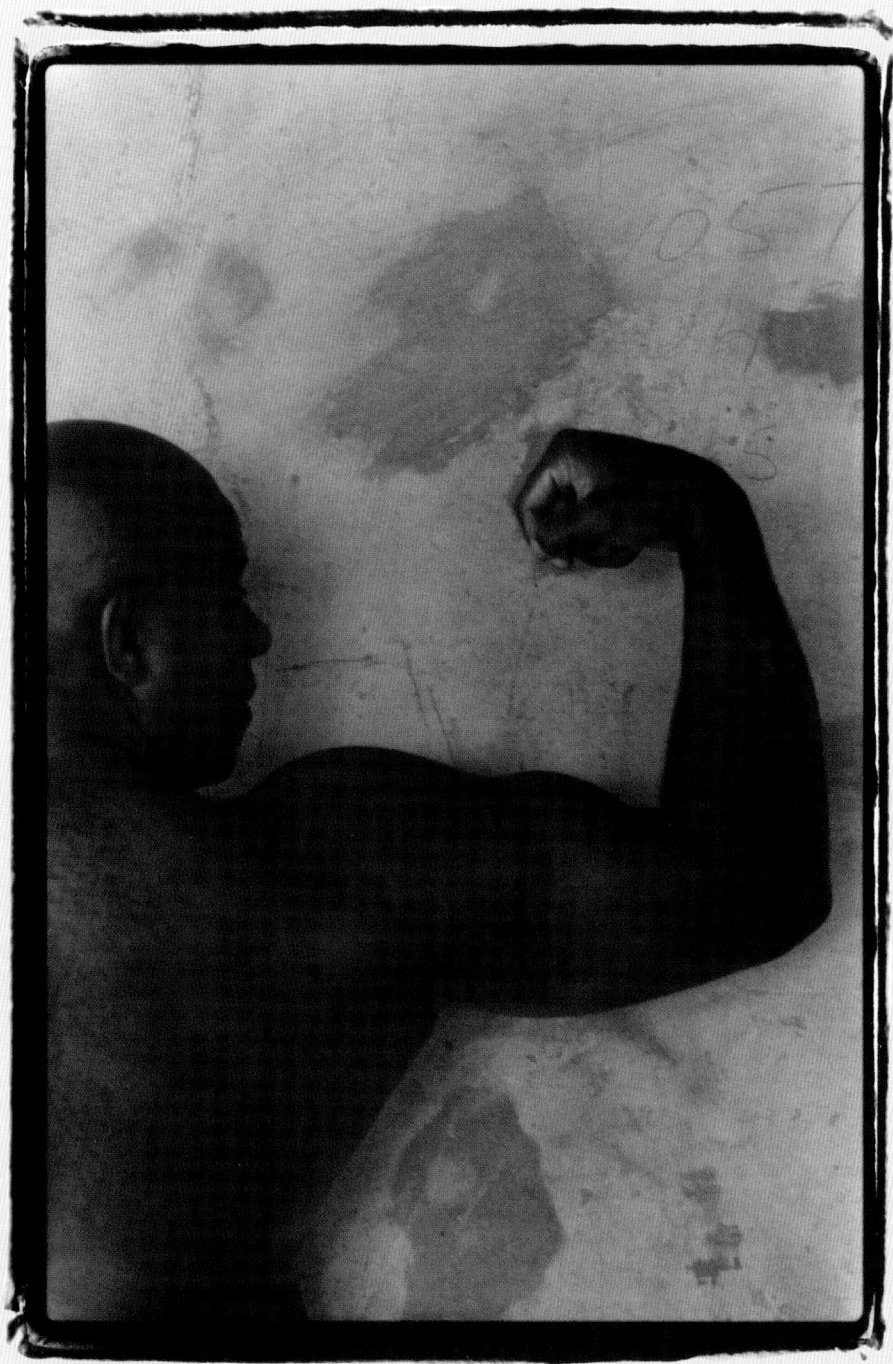

STRENGTHENING FOODS

Strengthening foods are protein foods.
I relish beans and pulses because they carry
properties that purify the body. I have also
included fish and shellfish dishes for active
people who need more flexibility with cooking
time. Beans and pulses stabilise and repair the
tissue, build muscle, provide endurance and are
essential for general vitality and wellbeing.

STRENGTHENING

BEAN ACTION

Apart from their excellent strengthening properties, new evidence also indicates that regular consumption of beans and pulses reduces the risk of cancer. Epidemiological studies (the study of diseases and their control and prevention) have identified substances in beans called 'protease inhibitors', which protect against the development of breast, stomach and skin tumours.

Eating beans or pulses helps contribute to the smooth functioning of the digestion, circulatory and nervous systems.

If you are feeling weak you should introduce strengthening foods into your diet.

COOKING BEANS

To improve digestibility most beans require soaking in water before cooking. Chickpeas, soya beans, azuki beans, pintos and kidney beans should be soaked for 2–6 hours or preferably overnight. If you are in a rush, soak the beans in hot water for half an hour. Cooking time varies between 1–2 hours depending on heat but beans should be soft enough when cooked to crush on your palate with your tongue. Lentils and other light beans require no soaking and only take $1/2$–1 hour to cook.

When cooking beans, add a strip of kombu seaweed to the bottom of the pot. This mineral-rich sea vegetable adds flavour to the beans and improves digestibility.

Always add salt or seasoning at the end of cooking. Seasonings include shoyu, miso and umeboshi vinegar.

SOYA BEANS WITH SPRING ONIONS ◗

Spring onions are small white onions that are harvested before the bulb has time to fully form. They are also known as scallions or green onions.

1 cup soya beans
1 strip kombu seaweed
1 tablespoon shoyu
1 cup spring onions, finely chopped
1 tablespoon lemon juice

◗ Soak soya beans in water for 6–12 hours. Rinse and cover with water in a pressure cooker or pot with kombu seaweed.
◗ Pressure cook on low heat for $1^1/4$ hours or simmer in pot for $1^3/4$ hours. Add shoyu and simmer for a further 2 minutes.
◗ Drain, place in a salad bowl and allow to cool.
◗ Add spring onions and lemon juice. Serve.

SOYA BEAN AND TOFU STIR-FRY ◗

Both tofu and soya beans are great proteins and offer strength to your body. With the richness of sesame oil, this stir-fry is delicious.

$1/2$ cup pumpkin, thinly sliced
$1/4$ cup carrots, cut into half moons
1 tablespoon sesame oil
1 block tofu, cut into 2 cm cubes
$1/4$ cup green capsicums, sliced into matchsticks
$1/4$ cup red capsicums, sliced into matchsticks
$1^1/2$ cups cooked soya beans
1 teaspoon shoyu
1 teaspoon brown rice vinegar

◗ Stir-fry pumpkin and carrots for 2 minutes in sesame oil then add tofu and stir-fry for 2 more minutes until golden. Add capsicum and stir-fry for another 2 minutes.
◗ Place soya beans in frying pan with shoyu and heat through for about 1 minute. Add brown rice vinegar and serve.

SOYA BEANS WITH GARLIC ▶

Soya beans rejuvenate body tissue. The highest-protein bean, soya helps to break down fat.

1 cup soya beans
1 strip kombu seaweed
1 tablespoon sesame oil
2 cloves garlic, finely diced
1 cup whole green beans
1 tablespoon tamari

▶ Soak soya beans for 6–12 hours with kombu seaweed.
▶ Bring soya beans to the boil and cook on medium heat with lid on for 1½ – 2 hours, keeping water level above beans. Remove, drain and place in a salad bowl.
▶ Heat sesame oil in a frying pan. Add garlic and green beans and sauté for 5 minutes with tamari. Add to soya beans and mix together evenly. Serve.

SOYA BEAN SALAD WITH SWEET MISO AND PARSLEY ▶

Studies show that soya beans aid in the healing process of diabetes, cirrhosis of the liver, and intestinal disorders and reduce the risk of cancer.

1 cup soya beans
1 strip kombu seaweed
1 tablespoon sweet white miso
1 cup parsley, finely chopped

▶ Soak soya beans for 6–12 hours and cook with kombu seaweed for 1½ – 2 hours until tender. Place in a salad bowl to cool.
▶ Add sweet rice miso and parsley. Serve.

SOYA BEANS WITH CARROTS ▶

The colour contrast of yellow soya beans and orange carrots makes this dish a visual delight. Both carrots and soya beans have healing properties that lower cholesterol and reduce the risk of disease. Soya beans are the most popular protein source in the world.

1 cup soya beans
1 strip kombu seaweed
2 tablespoons ginger, cut into small cubes
1 cup carrots, sliced into matchsticks
1½ teaspoons sunflower oil
1½ teaspoons miso
1 tablespoon water

▶ Soak soya beans and kombu seaweed for 6–12 hours.
▶ Pressure-cook beans and kombu seaweed for 1¼ hours with enough water to cover the beans. Remove, drain and place in a serving bowl.
▶ Sauté ginger and carrots with sunflower oil for 5 minutes. Add miso paste and water.
▶ Add to soya beans. Serve.

BEAN SALAD ▶

Use any combination of beans for this dish. Umeboshi has antioxidising properties and its sour flavour opens up tight organs to assist them in functioning correctly.

¹/₂ cup kidney beans
¹/₂ cup chickpeas
1 strip kombu seaweed
2 cups green beans
1 cup red onion, finely diced
1 tablespoon umeboshi vinegar
¹/₂ cup parsley

▶ Cook kidney beans and chickpeas with kombu seaweed (see p. 60 for cooking instructions).
▶ Steam green beans for 3 minutes.
▶ Mix together all ingredients and season with umeboshi vinegar. Garnish with parsley and serve.

CHICKPEA SALAD ▶

Chickpeas are good fluid absorbers, carrying excess fluid in the body through the intestines, taking the load off the kidneys.

1 cup chickpeas
1 strip kombu seaweed
2 cups leeks, thinly sliced
1 cup carrots, chopped into irregular chunks
1 tablespoon sesame oil
1 tablespoon shoyu
1 tablespoon brown rice vinegar

▶ Soak chickpeas for 3–6 hours. Rinse and cover with water and cook with kombu seaweed for 1¹/₄ hours. Drain then place in a serving bowl.
▶ Sauté leeks and carrots with sesame oil and shoyu for 20 minutes. Add brown rice vinegar.
▶ Mix vegetables with chickpeas. Serve.

CHICKPEAS WITH CARROTS AND ONIONS ▶

What a great combination for balancing abdominal swelling. The chickpeas absorb fluid and the onions cut fat. This dish is a great detoxifier.

1¹/₂ cups onions, sliced into rings
1 cup carrots, sliced into 2 cm rounds
³/₄ cup cucumber, cut into small cubes
1 teaspoon sesame oil
1 teaspoon tamari
1 can chickpeas

▶ Sauté vegetables in sesame oil for 5–6 minutes.
▶ Add chickpeas and tamari.
▶ Heat through for 2 minutes and serve.

CHICKPEAS WITH CARROTS AND CHIVES ▶

The contrast of colours in this dish makes your meal look great. Chickpeas continually absorb fluid. You'll notice that if you leave chickpeas to soak overnight in water they become dry. This action is what stimulates abdominal tone — the continual absorption of liquid in the intestines pulls the abdomen tight without dehydrating the blood.

1 cup carrots, cut into small cubes
2 cups cooked chickpeas
1 teaspoon tahini
1 tablespoon shoyu
1 tablespoon lemon juice
1 tablespoon water

▶ Blanch carrots and add to chickpeas.
▶ Mix together tahini, shoyu, lemon juice and water and fold into chickpeas and carrots.
▶ Garnish with chives and serve either hot or cold.

CHICKPEA, GARLIC AND TEMPEH STIR-FRY ▶

Tempeh is a great protein source made from soya beans, which makes this dish very strengthening.

1/4 cup arame seaweed
1/2 block tempeh, cut into 2 cm cubes
1/4 cup garlic, sliced
1 tablespoon sesame oil
1/2 cup spring onions, sliced into 4 cm long diagonals
1/2 cup yellow capsicum, cut into irregular pieces
1 1/2 cups cooked chickpeas
1 tablespoon shoyu
1 teaspoon brown rice vinegar

▶ Soak arame seaweed for 10–15 minutes then drain.
▶ Sauté garlic and tempeh in sesame oil for 5 minutes until golden then add spring onions, yellow capsicums and arame seaweed. Sauté for another 2–3 minutes.
▶ Add chickpeas, shoyu and brown rice vinegar. Heat through for 2 minutes and serve.

CHICKPEAS WITH CARAMELISED ONION ▶

This sweet dish is one of my favourites and another great way of using the sensational caramelised onions.

2 cups cooked chickpeas with kombu (see 'cooking beans' p. 60)
2 cups caramelised onions (see p.56)

▶ Mix chickpeas and caramelised onions together.
▶ Slice the kombu into thin strips and place decoratively on top. Serve.

HUMMUS ▌

Great on the side of your plate with rice, greens and a pressed salad or as traditionally used as a dip with crackers.

1 cup onions, diced
3 cloves garlic, diced
1 cup capsicum, cut into small cubes
1 teaspoon sesame oil
2 cups cooked chickpeas
2 cups water
1 teaspoon tahini
1 teaspoon shoyu
lemon juice
1 tablespoon chives

▌ Sauté the vegetables in sesame oil for 5 minutes then add cooked chickpeas and water and cook with lid on for a further 30 minutes on low heat.
▌ Add tahini, shoyu and lemon juice to taste then blend into a creamy consistency and garnish with chives. Serve.

BLACK BEANS, BUTTERBEANS AND WAKAME ▌

Wakame seaweed has antibacterial properties and black beans eliminate sugar and toxins from the intestines so this dish has exceptional qualities for healing the digestive system.

1 can washed and drained black beans (or cook as on p. 60)
$\frac{1}{2}$ cup wakame seaweed
4 spring onions, cut into 5 cm pieces
1 cup butterbeans, with ends cut off
1 teaspoon shoyu
1 teaspoon brown rice vinegar

▌ Rinse wakame seaweed and cut into 3 cm pieces.
▌ Heat 1 tablespoon water in a frying pan and sauté seaweed and vegetables for 3 minutes.
▌ Add beans and heat through for a further 2 minutes.
▌ Add shoyu and brown rice vinegar. Serve.

BLACK BEANS WITH CORN ▌

A great fuel for athletes. This small oval bean is a fantastic source of carbohydrate and is ideal for high energy users.

$1\frac{1}{2}$ cups cooked black beans
$\frac{1}{2}$ cup organic canned whole kernel sweetcorn
1 teaspoon shoyu
1 teaspoon brown rice vinegar

▌ Mix together all ingredients and serve.

AZUKI BEANS, BLACK BEANS AND CHICKPEAS ▶

Azuki beans tone the kidneys, black beans detoxify sugar and chickpeas help eliminate fluid retention. This powerful mixture is a great body-balancing dish.

½ cup azuki beans
½ cup black beans
½ cup chickpeas
1 strip kombu seaweed
4 cups water
2 teaspoons shoyu
2 teaspoons brown rice vinegar

▶ Place beans and chickpeas in pressure-cooker with kombu seaweed and grated ginger and cover with water.
▶ Pressure-cook for 1 hour.
▶ Allow pressure to return to normal then remove lid and add shoyu.
▶ Simmer for a further 2 minutes. Serve.

AZUKI BEANS WITH KOMBU AND PUMPKIN ▶

A powerful kidney-strengthening dish.

1 cup azuki beans
1 strip kombu seaweed
3 cups buttercup pumpkin, cut into chunks
3 cups water
1 tablespoon shoyu
½ cup grated ginger

▶ Soak azuki beans for 6–8 hours. Rinse and drain.
▶ Place kombu seaweed in a pot with azuki beans and pumpkin. Add water.
▶ Cover pot and cook on a medium-low heat for 1½ hours or until the beans are soft.
▶ Season mixture with shoyu and ginger and simmer for 5 minutes. Serve.

AZUKI BEANS WITH ONION ▶

The caramelised onions mixed with azuki beans give this dish a sweetness that tastes sensational.

2 cups cooked azuki beans (see 'cooking beans' p. 60)
1 cup caramelised onions (see p. 56)

▶ Mix together beans and onions and serve.

CLOCKWISE FROM LEFT: EXOTIC TONIC GREENS; BROWN RICE (P. 82);
AZUKI BEANS WITH ONION; PRESSED SPRING ONION AND CARROT (P. 26) ▶ ◗ ◗

CHESTNUT AZUKI STEW ▶

Chestnuts offer a rich body and creamy consistency and are powerful body-builders for anyone seeking more vitality. They are also great for the skin and for eliminating cellulite.

1 cup azuki beans
¹⁄₂ cup dried chestnuts
1 strip kombu seaweed
¹⁄₂ cup spring onions, finely chopped
¹⁄₂ cup carrots, sliced into matchsticks
2 teaspoons miso

▶ Soak azuki beans with chestnuts for 3–8 hours.
▶ Cover with water, bring to the boil with kombu seaweed and simmer for 1¹⁄₄ hours with the lid on.
▶ Add spring onions, carrots and miso paste mixed with hot water into a smooth consistency.
▶ Simmer for a further 5 minutes or until water has evaporated and chestnuts and azuki beans have thickened.

AZUKI BEANS WITH RAW VEGETABLES ▶

The raw vegetables and dressing make this dish unique. Azuki beans are very powerful for giving the body strength but sometimes need lightening up to be appetising.

1 tablespoon lemon juice
1 teaspoon seed mustard
1 tablespoon brown rice vinegar
1 teaspoon flaxseed oil
1 cup cucumber, with seeds removed and chopped into small cubes
¹⁄₂ cup spring onions, finely sliced on the diagonal
1 cup celery, finely sliced on the diagonal
2 cups cooked azuki beans

▶ Mix liquids and mustard, then add to vegetables and azuki beans. Mix well and serve cold.

AZUKI BEANS WITH TOFU ▶

Be creative with cutting styles. The different shapes and sizes make quite a difference to your dish.

1 block tofu, chopped
1 cup courgettes, chopped
¹⁄₂ cup carrots, chopped
¹⁄₂ cup onions, sliced
1 teaspoon sunflower oil
1 teaspoon shoyu
1 teaspoon brown rice vinegar
1 cup cooked azuki beans

▶ Sauté tofu and vegetables with sunflower oil for 5 minutes or until crispy.
▶ Add shoyu and brown rice vinegar, then mix in a salad bowl with azuki beans. Serve hot or cold.

PINTO BEANS WITH PUMPKIN AND KUMARA ▶

The ginger helps activate sluggish metabolisms and adds a terrific flavour to the beans.

1 cup pumpkin, cut into 1 cm cubes
1 cup kumara, cut into 1 cm cubes
2 cups cooked pinto beans
1 tablespoon lemon juice
¹/₄ cup grated ginger, squeezed to make 1 tablespoon ginger juice
1 tablespoon sesame seaweed shake
1 tablespoon tamari
¹/₂ cup spring onions

▶ Boil pumpkin and kumara for 10 minutes. Add to cooked pinto beans.
▶ Mix lemon juice, squeezed ginger juice, sesame seaweed shake and tamari together and pour over pinto beans and vegetables.
▶ Garnish with spring onions. Serve.

PINTO BEANS, TOFU AND CARROTS ▶

Pinto beans and tofu cooked this way are a fantastic source of carbohydrate and energy fuel for athletes.

1 block tofu, cut into 2 cm cubes
1 can pinto beans
³/₄ cup carrot sticks
2 teaspoons mugi miso
Squeeze of fresh grated ginger root

▶ Heat pinto beans, tofu and carrot in a saucepan for 3 minutes with ¹/₄ cup water.
▶ Mix miso and ginger with 1 teaspoon hot water then add to saucepan.
▶ Simmer for 2–3 minutes. Serve.

PINTO BEANS WITH MISO ▶

If beans aren't cooked for the appropriate length of time they will be toxic and can give you flatulence.

1 cup pinto beans
1 strip kombu seaweed
1 cup carrots, cut into irregular chunks
1 cup broccoli, cut into small florets
1 tablespoon miso
1 teaspoon flaxseed oil
1 tablespoon seed mustard

▶ Soak pinto beans for 3–6 hours, rinse with cold water and then cook with a strip of kombu seaweed for 1¹/₄ hours on a medium heat with lid on. Drain and place into a salad bowl.
▶ Boil carrots and broccoli for 5 minutes then add to chickpeas.
▶ Mix miso with 2 tablespoons of hot water, flaxseed oil and seed mustard before adding to vegetables and pinto beans. Serve.

RED LENTIL DISH ▶

The combination of red lentils, garlic and onions makes this dish a great fat dissolver and body purifier.

1 cup onions, diced
3 cloves garlic, finely chopped
1 cup red lentils
1 strip kombu seaweed
1 teaspoon miso

▶ Place onion and garlic in the bottom of a pot.
▶ Wash lentils and kombu and add to the pot. Cover with water and cook for 35–40 minutes – keep topping up with cold water as necessary to prevent burning. Stir frequently.
▶ Mix miso with a small amount of the cooking liquid and then add to the pot. Cook for a further 5 minutes. Serve.

TOFU AND CORN DISH ▶

Although tofu is not a strong protein, its texture is divine. By using the canned corn, this style of cooking is fast.

1 block tofu, cut into 1 cm slices
1 tablespoon shoyu
1 tablespoon sesame oil
1x 425 gram can whole kernel organic corn
³⁄₄ cup spring onions, finely sliced
¹⁄₄ cup parsley
¹⁄₂ cup basil or rocket

▶ Marinate tofu in shoyu for 5 minutes.
▶ Fry tofu for approximately 5 minutes in sesame oil until both sides are crisp.
▶ Open can of corn and pour over tofu. Heat mixture through for 2 minutes then add spring onions, parsley and basil or rocket.
▶ Cook for 2 minutes. Serve.

FRIED TOFU ▶

A texture delight that is high in protein.

1 block tofu, cut into triangles
1 teaspoon shoyu
1 tablespoon sesame oil

▶ Heat oil in frying pan and place tofu into the hot oil.
▶ Crisp both sides of tofu (it takes a couple of minutes per side).
▶ Splash tofu with shoyu. Serve hot.

FRIED TOFU WITH SEED MUSTARD ◗

The seed mustard helps the liver digest the oil.

1 block tofu, thinly sliced
1 tablespoon sesame oil
1 teaspoon seed mustard
1 teaspoon tamari

◗ Fry tofu in sesame oil for 3 minutes per side or until crispy.
◗ Spread cooked tofu with mustard and add a splash of tamari.

FRIED TOFU WITH SPRING ONIONS ◗

A favourite of mine when I've had a big day and don't feel like cooking for too long. It is quick to prepare and gives me strength. Tofu is also one protein that doesn't take long to digest, so you can eat it late at night without upsetting the digestion.

¹/₂ block tofu, chopped into cubes
¹/₂ cup spring onions, sliced finely on the diagonal
1 teaspoon sesame oil
1 teaspoon shoyu
1 teaspoon brown rice vinegar

◗ Toss tofu and spring onions in a frying pan or wok with sesame oil and shoyu for 5 minutes.
◗ Add brown rice vinegar and serve.

BOILED TOFU ◗

Tofu or soya bean curd is a textural delight. Its delicate consistency offers you an easily digested protein that takes no time to prepare. This boiled tofu dish is a great way of eating proteins without fats or oils.

1 block tofu
1 teaspoon shoyu
1 teaspoon seed mustard
1 teaspoon flaxseed oil
1 teaspoon brown rice vinegar

◗ Cover tofu block with water and boil for 5 minutes. Remove and slice into triangles.
◗ Mix shoyu, mustard, flaxseed oil and brown rice vinegar in a cup and pour over tofu.

OYSTERS WITH DRESSING (P. 78) ◗ ◗ ◗

FRIED TEMPEH ▶

Fried tempeh is rich and satisfying. It provides great fuel for physically active people who don't have a lot of time for preparing a meal.

1 block tempeh, cut in long slices
1 tablespoon sesame oil
1 teaspoon shoyu
1 teaspoon seed mustard

▶ In a frying pan heat sesame oil and gently fry tempeh until golden on both sides – about 5 minutes each side.
▶ Remove and flavour with shoyu and seed mustard.

TEMPEH WITH GINGER ▶

Tempeh is a soya bean cake that has been fermented to create a high-enzyme protein. A power fuel that offers great strength to vegans, organic tempeh is free of genetic modification, chemicals and poisons.

1 strip kombu seaweed
1 block tempeh
1 tablespoon ginger, sliced
1 tablespoon tamari

▶ Place kombu seaweed on bottom of pot and add tempeh. Cover with water.
▶ Bring to the boil and simmer for 15–20 mintues with lid on.

BARBECUED FLOUNDER ▶

Fresh flounder on the barbecue provides a healthy alternative to sausages.

1 wooden skewer
1 flounder
$^1/_2$ cup spring onions, finely chopped
juice of 1 lemon

▶ Stick skewer through flounder and place on the barbecue. Cook for 2 minutes each side or until fish is cooked.
▶ Mix spring onions with lemon juice in a cup. Pour over cooked flounder and serve.

MUSSEL AND PIPI BOIL-UP ▶

Fresh New Zealand seafood is a powerful strengthening food.

¹/₂ cup celery, finely chopped
3 garlic cloves, finely chopped
¹/₂ cup spring onions, finely chopped
2 cups mussels
1 cup pipis
1 tablespoon brown rice vinegar

▶ Add celery, garlic and spring onions to a pot with plenty of water and bring to the boil.
▶ Add mussels, pipis and brown rice vinegar and boil with a lid on until the shellfish open – about 2–3 minutes.
▶ Serve in a bowl with cooking liquid and enjoy both seafood and liquid.

OYSTERS WITH DRESSING ▶

A sensual delight. The ultimate aphrodisiac.

1 dozen fresh oysters in shell
1 tablespoon fresh dill
1 tablespoon olive oil
1 teaspoon balsamic vinegar
1 tablespoon lemon juice
1 teaspoon shoyu
1 tablespoon water

▶ Place fresh oysters on ice.
▶ Mix together all remaining ingredients and sprinkle over oysters. Enjoy.

TUNA STEAK ▶

Tuna is low in fat and is a powerful sexual libido fuel. It provides strength to the living cell.

1 teaspoon sesame oil
1 tuna steak

▶ Heat sesame oil in a frying pan and cook tuna steak on both sides until golden, about 2 minutes per side.
▶ Serve with carrot press, exotic tonic greens and boiled rice for a quick four-level balanced meal.

TONING FOODS

Grains have served as humankind's principal food
for thousands of years. The different types of
grain, farming methods, and creative cooking
styles have given rise to a wonderful diversity and
richness in the earth's cultures and societies.
The toning action of grains provides resilience
and fullness to the living cell, which completes
the circle of balance of the four levels of food.

TONING

Toning grains include amaranth, short and long grain brown rice, quinoa, millet, buckwheat and barley.

COOKING GRAINS

To obtain the best out of your grain dishes, follow the cooking suggestions below.

Remember to add a pinch of organic sea salt per cup of grain when cooking. Salt acts as a catalyst in the digestion of grain and makes it more alkaline when cooked, which helps the performance of the intestines.

Grain is a very hard food and to cook it evenly the high pressure and heat of a pressure cooker is preferable. Grain cooked by a conventional method can be cooked on the outside but still raw on the inside, or cooked on the inside and mushy and sticky on the outside.

However, it is fine if cooked on a low heat with the lid on.

The following recipes can be prepared in a pot with the lid on, or with pressure or rice cookers.

AMARANTH

Use 1 cup of grain to every $1^3/_4$ cups of water. Cook covered for 20 minutes on a low heat.

AMARANTH 20% / SHORT GRAIN BROWN RICE 80%

Use 1 cup of this mixture to every 2 cups of water. Cook covered for 30–45 minutes on a low heat with a lid on the pot.

BARLEY

Use 1 cup to every 2 cups of water. Cook covered for 30–45 minutes on a low heat.

BUCKWHEAT

Use 1 cup to every $1^1/_2$ cups of water. Cook for 20–30 minutes on a low heat.

MILLET

Ensure you buy hulled millet. Use 1 cup to every 2 cups of water. Cook for 30–45 minutes on a low heat.

QUINOA

Use 1 cup to every $1^3/_4$ cups of water. Bring the mixture to the boil and simmer for 10 minutes. Turn off the heat and leave for 10 minutes before removing from the pot.

QUINOA 20% / SHORT GRAIN BROWN RICE 80%

Use 1 cup of mixture to every $1^3/_4$ cups of water. Cook covered for 30–45 minutes on a low heat with a lid on the pot.

LONG AND SHORT GRAIN BROWN RICE

Use 1 cup to every 2 cups of water. Cook for 30–45 minutes on a low heat with a lid on the pot.

RICE WITH BASIL ◗

Cultivated worldwide, basil is an annual plant with healing properties. You can boil basil leaves with 2 cups of water and use the tea for headaches, migraines, restless sleep or even to stimulate milk production for breast-feeding mothers.

$^1/_2$ cup carrots, cut into matchsticks
$^1/_2$ cup courgettes, cut into half moons
$^1/_2$ cup spring onions, sliced finely on a diagonal
$^1/_2$ cup basil
1 tablespoon sunflower oil
2 cups cooked brown rice
1 tablespoon shoyu
1 tablespoon brown rice vinegar

◗ Sauté vegetables with sunflower oil for 3 minutes.
◗ Add rice and shoyu and sauté for a further 3 minutes. Add brown rice vinegar and serve hot.

RICE WITH PINE NUTS ◗

Pine nuts are great for the skin. Oily to say the least, the fine delicate qualities of this nut permeate the tissue wall and rejuvenate the skin without creating a congested oil secretion that causes pimples.

2 cups cooked short grain brown rice
1 cup courgettes, cut into irregular chunks
1 tablespoon balsamic vinegar
1 cup pine nuts

◗ Place cooked rice in a salad bowl.
◗ Blanch courgettes. Add to rice and flavour with balsamic vinegar.
◗ Wash pine nuts and roast in a frying pan for 5 minutes until golden brown.
◗ Add to salad and serve.

RICE, MILLET AND CAULIFLOWER ◗

Millet and cauliflower are rich and creamy and go well with rice. This dish is great for the lymphatic system.

1 cup short grain brown rice
$^1/_2$ cup millet
3 cups water
pinch sea salt
2 cups cauliflower, large florets

◗ Mix short grain brown rice with millet and water. Place in a pressure-cooker or large pot with sea salt.
◗ Place cauliflower on top of rice/millet mixture.
◗ Cook the mixture for 45 minutes.
◗ Place in a serving bowl.

RICE, MUSHROOOMS AND TOFU ▶

Mushrooms have grown for thousands of years in Europe and Asia and have been cultivated for the last three centuries. There are 250 edible varieties available worldwide, with the most common New Zealand varieties including button, open, flat, oyster, and shitake.

1 cup brown rice
2 cups water
pinch sea salt
¹/₂ cup mushrooms, cut into chunks
1 teaspoon sesame oil
1 teaspoon tamari
¹/₂ block tofu, sliced into long fingers
1 teaspoon brown rice vinegar

▶ Place rice in a pressure-cooker or pot with water. Add sea salt and pressure-cook for 34–45 minutes or boil for 45–55 minutes. When cooked, allow to cool and place rice in a serving dish.
▶ Sauté mushrooms with sesame oil and tamari for 5 minutes in a wok or frying pan.
▶ Add tofu to the vegetables. Sauté mixture for another 5 minutes and then add to rice.
▶ Splash mixed ingredients with brown rice vinegar. Serve.

RICE LOAF WITH CARROTS AND SPRING ONIONS ▶

Rice loaves are easy to prepare and can be made from any combination of rice grain and vegetables. They can be sliced or fried or eaten with hummus or any spread. They are ideal for lunch and a great way of being organised for the next day.

1¹/₂ cups carrots or spring onions or a mix of both, cut into fine matchsticks
3 cups cooked short grain brown rice
1 tablespoon brown rice vinegar

▶ Blanch carrots. Mix with spring onions, rice and brown rice vinegar.
▶ Press mixture with slightly wet hand into a loaf tin or glass container until firm.
▶ Leave to set for half an hour then turn over to remove from container. Slice and enjoy.

PRESSURE-COOKED BROWN RICE WITH AZUKI BEANS ▶

The combination of rice and beans adds strengthening and toning qualities to the one dish.

¹/₄ cup azuki beans
1 cup brown rice
pinch sea salt

▶ Wash beans, place in a pot and cover with water. Bring to the boil and cook on a medium-low heat for 15 minutes.
▶ Place washed rice in the pressure-cooker. Add beans and 2 cups of water.
▶ Add sea salt, cover, turn to high heat and then reduce to a medium-low heat and cook for 50 minutes. Serve.

RICE AND AMARANTH SAUTÉ ▶

Amaranth is the 'tummy toner' as it strongly tightens the peristaltic muscles of the intestinal wall.

1 cup brown rice
1 cup amaranth
pinch sea salt
3¹/₂ cups water
2 cloves garlic, diced
¹/₂ cup spring onion, sliced on a diagonal
¹/₂ cup capsicum, cut into chunks
1 tablespoon sesame oil
1 tablespoon tomato basil purée
1 teaspoon brown rice vinegar

▶ Mix rice and amaranth with water and sea salt. Cook with lid on for half an hour. Remove from heat and allow to cool.
▶ Sauté garlic, spring onions and capsicum in the sesame oil for 10 minutes.
▶ Add other ingredients to the vegetable mixture, sauté for a further 5 minutes and serve hot.

RICE AND AMARANTH BALLS ▶

Any grain can be made into these delicious convenient balls. Try frying in sesame oil or on the barbecue.

4 cups cooked brown rice and amaranth (see p. 82 for cooking instructions)

▶ Using both hands, firmly press together the cooked rice and amaranth into oval-shaped balls.

RICE, QUINOA AND TOFU ▶

Flaxseed oil adds a lovely flavour and is a good source of Omega 3, which aids digestion and improves skin condition.

1 cup short grain brown rice
¹/₄ cup quinoa
2¹/₄ cups water
pinch sea salt
1 block tofu, cut into cubes
¹/₂ cup courgettes, sliced into strips
¹/₂ cup whole mushrooms
1 tablespoon flaxseed oil
1 tablespoon tamari
1 teaspoon brown rice vinegar

▶ Mix rice and quinoa. Add water and sea salt and cook for 40 minutes. Place cooked grain in a salad bowl to cool.
▶ Boil tofu, carrots and courgettes for 5 minutes with mushrooms. Place cooked vegetables with the grain mixture in the salad bowl.
▶ Add flaxseed oil, tamari and brown rice vinegar to flavour and then fold all ingredients evenly. Serve.

RICE AND BROCCOLI SALAD ❱

Broccoli was first cultivated in Italy in the 16th century. Broccoli means 'little sprouts' in Italian and is part of the health-giving brassica family.

2 cups cooked brown rice
1 cup onions, diced
2 cloves garlic, cut into small cubes
1 tablespoon sesame oil
1 tablespoon shoyu
1 cup broccoli, small florets
1 cup cauliflower, small florets
1 cup kumara, cut into 2 cm cubes
1 tablespoon seed mustard

❱ Place cooked rice in a salad bowl.
❱ Sauté onions and garlic with sesame oil and shoyu for 10 minutes. Add to rice.
❱ Add vegetables to boiling water and cook for 5 minutes. Drain and add vegetables to rice.
❱ Mix seed mustard into the rice salad. Serve.

RICE WITH CABBAGE ❱

Cabbages are thought to have originated in Asia and the eastern Mediterranean. They are one of the oldest vegetables and were long considered food for the poor. There are many varieties of cabbage with the one best known to us — the firm-headed variety — first appearing around the 16th century.

2 cups cooked brown rice
1 cup cabbage, finely shredded
1 tablespoon sesame oil
1 tablespoon tamari
1 tablespoon brown rice vinegar
1 tablespoon grated ginger

❱ Place cooked rice into a salad bowl.
❱ Sauté cabbage in sesame oil for 5 minutes. Flavour with tamari, brown rice vinegar and ginger.
❱ Mix rice and cabbage mixture together well. Serve.

RICE AND HERB MIX ❱

Light and easy, fresh garden herbs add a whole new dimension to rice dishes. A clean, light rice salad.

1 tablespoon fresh herbs
1 cup cooked brown rice
1 teaspoon brown rice vinegar

❱ Chop fresh herbs finely and mix with cooked rice in a salad bowl. Add brown rice vinegar. Serve.

RICE, SPRING ONION AND COURGETTE STIR-FRY ▶

When cooking rice it is more efficient to prepare extra to use for other meals, such as stir-fries. Place extra rice in a sealed container in the fridge where it will last for up to 3 days.

1 teaspoon sesame oil
¹/₂ cup tofu, cut into cubes
¹/₂ cup spring onions, finely chopped on a diagonal
¹/₂ cup courgettes, cut into irregular chunks
1 cup cooked brown rice
1 teaspoon shoyu
1 teaspoon rice vinegar

▶ Heat sesame oil in a frying pan and sauté tofu, courgettes and spring onions for 3 minutes.
▶ Add rice and sauté for a further 3 minutes and season with shoyu and brown rice vinegar.

EASY RICE STIR-FRY ▶

Quick and tasty.

1 teaspoon sesame oil
1 cup leeks, finely sliced
¹/₂ cup courgettes, cut into irregular chunks
1¹/₂ cups cooked brown rice
1 teaspoon tamari
1 teaspoon brown rice vinegar

▶ Heat oil in frying pan and toss leeks for 5 minutes, then add courgettes and cooked rice. Stir-fry the mixture for a further 5 minutes, then season with tamari and brown rice vinegar. Serve.

WHITE RICE STIR-FRY ▶

White rice was once the preserve of the oriental élite as it was obtained by hand-peeling the outer brown layer from brown rice.

1 cup short grain white rice
pinch sea salt
1³/₄ cups water
1 cup courgettes, sliced
3 cloves garlic, cut into small cubes
1 tablespoon sesame oil
1 tablespoon tomato paste
1 tablespoon shoyu

▶ Cook rice in water and sea salt for 20 minutes and then allow to cool.
▶ Sauté courgettes and garlic in sesame oil.
▶ Add tomato paste and shoyu to the vegetables.
▶ Mix together rice and vegetables and serve either hot or cold.

SUSHI ▶

Sushi means 'vinegared rice' and is traditionally made with whole brown rice, brown rice vinegar and nori seaweed. Maki-sushi is the familiar rolled sushi in which cooked rice is layered with vegetables, fish or pickles, wrapped in toasted nori and sliced into rounds.

1 cup carrot, cut into thin matchsticks
1 cup cucumber, sliced lengthwise into strips 1 cm thick
2 sheets toasted nori seaweed
2 cups cooked organic white rice
1 teaspoon brown rice vinegar
1 tablespoon pickled ginger
1 tablespoon shoyu

- ▶ Blanch and cool vegetables.
- ▶ Place a sheet of toasted nori on a bamboo sushi mat. Evenly spread rice over the nori sheet, leaving 2.5 cm at the top edge and 1 cm on the bottom edge uncovered.
- ▶ Press rice down firmly with a slightly damp hand.
- ▶ Place cucumber and carrot across the width of the nori sheet 2.5 cm from the bottom and sprinkle with brown rice vinegar.
- ▶ Use both hands to roll the sushi mat into a cylinder shape, pressing mat firmly against nori and rice. When nori sheet is completely rolled up, wet top edge lightly with water and press to seal edges tightly.
- ▶ Before unrolling the sushi mat, squeeze gently to remove excess liquid.
- ▶ Wet a sharp knife and slice nori roll into small rounds.
- ▶ Arrange sushi on a plate with pickled ginger and shoyu.

SUSHI WITH TEMPEH ▶

Many types of nori grow wild in different parts of the world. It is called 'laver' in Wales, 'sloke' in Ireland, 'slake' in Scotland and 'black butter' in Devon and was traditionally served as a condiment with oats. In New Zealand it is called karengo. Sushi nori is cultivated and prepared into sheets in the Far East.

1 block tempeh
3 sheets toasted nori
3 cups cooked brown rice
1 teaspoon mustard

- ▶ Heat sesame oil in a frying pan and crisp tempeh for about 2 minutes each side.
- ▶ Make sushi as instructed above, placing tempeh lengthwise and spreading with mustard.

MILLET WITH BROWN RICE VINEGAR ▶

Millet is the most alkalising grain and helps build immunity.

1 cup millet
1 teaspoon brown rice vinegar
1 tablespoon chives, finely sliced

▶ Simmer millet in 2 cups of water for 30–40 minutes with the lid on.
▶ Place in bowl with brown rice vinegar and garnish with chives.

AMARANTH WITH ONIONS ▶

This rich dish is a favourite of those who attend my classes. The sweetness of sautéed onions and the richness of tamari are a great way of introducing this powerful abdominal toner – amaranth.

1 cup amaranth
2 cups onions, sliced
1 tablespoon sesame oil
1 tablespoon tamari
1 tablespoon fresh ginger juice

▶ Mix amaranth with $1\frac{1}{2}$ cups of water and a pinch of salt. Boil with lid on for 20 minutes. Allow to cool.
▶ Sauté onions with sesame oil for 15 minutes in frying pan.
▶ Add tamari, ginger juice and amaranth then heat through for 2-3 minutes. Serve.

AMARANTH WITH SPRING ONIONS AND ARAME ▶

With its seed-like qualities, amaranth activates energy reserves trapped inside a tired body. Spring onions cut fat and arame is known for lowering blood pressure and is a great source of calcium for the bones.

$\frac{1}{2}$ cup arame seaweed
2 cups spring onions, cut into 1 cm pieces
1 teaspoon sunflower oil
1 teaspoon tamari
1 cup cooked amaranth
1 teaspoon brown rice vinegar

▶ Soak arame seaweed for 10 minutes.
▶ Sauté drained arame and spring onions in sunflower oil for 5 minutes.
▶ Add tamari and amaranth and sauté for a further 3 minutes.
▶ Add brown rice vinegar. Serve.

CLOCKWISE FROM TOP: GREEN SALAD WITH FLAXSEED OIL (P. 42); PRESSED CELERY AND COURGETTE SALAD (P. 28); AMARANTH WITH ONIONS; CHICKPEAS WITH CARROTS AND ONIONS (P. 63) ▶ ▶ ▶

AMARANTH WITH COURGETTES AND CARROTS ▶

Quick and easy, light and fresh, you can use any vegetable with this dish, so be creative.

¹/₂ cup carrots, cut into matchsticks
1 cup courgettes, cut into matchsticks
2 cups cooked amaranth
1 tablespoon lemon juice
1 teaspoon sesame seaweed shake

▶ Blanch carrots and courgettes.
▶ Add vegetables to amaranth and season with lemon juice. Mix evenly and garnish with sesame seaweed shake. Serve.

QUINOA SALAD ▶

Quinoa is the highest protein grain and is known for its healing power.

1 cup quinoa
1¹/₂ cups water
¹/₄ teaspoon sea salt
¹/₂ cup courgettes, cut into long strips
¹/₂ block tofu, cut into cubes
1 teaspoon flaxseed oil
1 teaspoon tamari
1 teaspoon brown rice vinegar
1 teaspoon seed mustard

▶ Cook quinoa with water and sea salt for 10 minutes on a very low heat. Turn the heat off and leave in the pan with the lid on for 5 minutes before placing in a salad bowl.
▶ Blanch courgettes and tofu for 2 minutes. Drain and add to the quinoa.
▶ Mix flaxseed oil, tamari, brown rice vinegar and seed mustard with 1 tablespoon of water and fold into the salad. Serve.

QUINOA WITH CARROTS AND TOFU ▶

You get a double protein hit from the tofu and quinoa, so this makes for a great lunch or dinner when you don't have a lot of time.

1 cup carrots, cut into fine matchsticks
1 block tofu, cut into small triangles
1 teaspoon seed mustard
1 teaspoon flaxseed oil
1 teaspoon shoyu
1 teaspoon lemon juice
1¹/₂ cups cooked quinoa

▶ Boil carrots and tofu for 3 minutes.
▶ Place in a salad bowl and season with seed mustard, flaxseed oil, shoyu, lemon juice and a little water.
▶ Mix together vegetables and cooked quinoa. Serve.

BARLEY WITH ORANGE AND PUMPKIN ▶

Barley has long been known for its healing properties for the liver and also as a great fat dissolver. With the fluid-absorbing qualities of pumpkin, this makes a great dish for balance and body tone.

1 cup pumpkin, cut into 2 cm pieces
2 cups cooked barley
1/2 cup celery, finely sliced
1/2 cup orange juice
1 teaspoon lemon zest

▶ Boil pumpkin for 5 minutes then add to cooked barley.
▶ Blanch celery for 3 minutes and add with orange juice to barley and pumpkin.
▶ Garnish with lemon zest. Serve.

MILLET WITH MUNG BEAN SPROUTS AND CARROTS ▶

Millet is the most alkalising grain. It is known for its powerful ability to build strength into the immune system.

1 cup carrots, cut into matchsticks
2 cups cooked hulled millet
1 cup mung bean sprouts
1 teaspoon brown rice vinegar

▶ Blanch carrots and place in a salad bowl with all other ingredients. Mix together and serve.

MILLET CROQUETTES ▶

Millett has a creamy quality and sweet flavours. Its creamy consistency helps the croquettes to hold together well.

2 cups hulled millet
3 1/2 cups water
pinch sea salt
1/2 cup red capsicum, diced
1/2 cup onions, diced
1 tablespoon sesame oil
1 tablespoon shoyu

▶ Wash millet and place in a pot with water and sea salt. Bring to the boil and simmer for 30 minutes with the lid on. Remove and allow to cool.
▶ Mix capsicum and onion thoroughly with cooked millet.
▶ With wet hands form the mixture into firmly packed balls, using approximately half a cup of mixture per ball. Flatten balls into croquettes.
▶ Heat sesame oil in frying pan on a medium heat. Fry croquettes until golden brown and crisp on both sides.
▶ Remove croquettes from heat and season with shoyu. Serve.

BARLEY STIR-FRY ▶

Quick and easy, barley can be made into interesting stir-fry dishes in the same way as rice.

¹/₂ cup red capsicum, finely sliced
1 cup courgettes, cut into irregular chunks
¹/₄ cup fresh ginger, cut into matchsticks
1 teaspoon sesame oil
1 teaspoon shoyu
1¹/₂ cups cooked barley

▶ Sauté vegetables for 3 minutes in sesame oil.
▶ Add shoyu and cooked barley. Serve.

BARLEY WITH PUMPKIN ▶

Barley is an uplifting grain that helps the liver to balance the blood.

1 cup barley
1 tablespoon lemon zest, finely sliced
¹/₄ teaspoon sea salt
2 cups pumpkin, cut into irregular chunks

▶ Pressure-cook barley in 1¹/₂ cups of water with lemon zest and sea salt for 40–50 minutes.
▶ When pressure has been released place barley in a serving dish and allow to cool.
▶ Boil pumpkin for 5 minutes or until cooked then add to barley.

BARLEY WITH MUSHROOMS

Smooth and creamy, this barley dish is sensational.

¹/₂ cup onions, diced
1 cup button mushrooms, halved
2 cloves garlic, finely sliced
1 teaspoon sesame oil
1 teaspoon shoyu
2 cups cooked barley

▶ Sauté onions, mushrooms and garlic in sesame oil for 3 minutes then add shoyu and sauté for a further 2 minutes.
▶ Add mixuture to barley and serve hot or cold.

BARLEY WITH PUMPKIN; EXOTIC TONIC GREENS (P. 38); CHICKPEA, GARLIC AND
TEMPEH STIR-FRY (P. 64); PRESSED RED ONION AND CUCUMBER SALAD (P. 26)   ▶ ▶ ▶

BREAKFAST

SOUP

FUEL FOOD

DESSERT

BREAKFAST FOODS

MILLET PORRIDGE ❱

A smooth and creamy porridge. Millet is powerful for strengthening the immune system and alkalising the blood.

³⁄₄ cup hulled millet
¹⁄₄ cup raisins
3 cups water
1 pear, finely sliced
pinch sea salt
1 tablespoon soya milk

❱ Place millet, raisins, water and sea salt in a pot. Simmer for 40 minutes then leave overnight with heat turned off.
❱ Steam pear for 5 minutes.
❱ Serve millet porridge in a bowl with pear and soya milk on top.

MILLET PORRIDGE WITH RASPBERRY JAM ❱

Millet porridge is alkalising and healing for the immune system.

1 cup cooked hulled millet
1 cup water
1 teaspoon brown rice malt
1 tablespoon yoghurt
¹⁄₂ kiwifruit, sliced
1 tablespoon raspberry jam
3 grapes
1 sprig fennel

❱ Simmer cooked millet and water for 30 minutes. Stir frequently to avoid lumps.
❱ Serve in a bowl with brown rice malt, raspberry jam, yoghurt and fruit then garnish with fennel.

RICE PORRIDGE ❱

This porridge is light and clean and has a great quality for toning the abdomen.

1 cup cooked brown rice
1¹⁄₂ cups water
1 teaspoon flaxseed oil
1 teaspoon shoyu
1 tablespoon roasted sunflower seeds

❱ Simmer cooked rice with water for 15 minutes. Stir frequently. Leave overnight in pot with heat turned off.
❱ Reheat in the morning and serve in bowl with flaxseed oil, shoyu and sunflower seeds.

APPLE AND RICE PORRIDGE ▶

Use the Ceres organic rice cereal as it is made from oven-roasted Demeter certified brown rice.

2 apples, cored and cut into small chunks
zest from 1/4 lemon
1/4 cup raisins
3/4 cup organic rice cereal
pinch sea salt
1 teaspoon maple syrup
rice milk

▶ Place apples in saucepan with lemon zest and raisins. Add water to almost cover mixture and simmer for 10 minutes.
▶ In a separate pot add rice cereal, sea salt and 2½ cups water. Cover and simmer for 5 minutes. Remove from the heat and stir until smooth.
▶ Add stewed fruit, maple syrup and rice milk for flavour.

BARLEY PORRIDGE ▶

This porridge is creamy and opens up the liver for cleansing the blood.

1 cup cooked barley
1 teaspoon lemon zest
1 tablespoon raisins
1½ cups water
1 tablespoon soya milk
1 teaspoon maple syrup

▶ Simmer cooked barley, lemon zest and raisins in water for 15 minutes. Leave overnight in pot with heat turned off.
▶ Reheat in the morning and serve in bowl with soya milk and maple syrup.

SOAKED MUESLI AND APPLE PURÉE ▶

An energising breakfast. Soaking the muesli ferments the grains, activating the essential enzymes that open up and energise the liver.

3/4 cup muesli
1½ cups rice milk
2 apples
1 cup water
1 teaspoon brown rice malt

▶ Soak muesli overnight in your breakfast bowl with rice milk.
▶ The same evening, boil cored and chopped apples with water for 10 minutes. Add brown rice malt and allow to cool overnight.
▶ The following morning, place the apple purée into your soaked muesli and enjoy.

SOFT RICE CEREAL ▶

This creamy rice cereal is great for creating perfect food balance because it is so easy to digest. I prefer cooking it at night and eating it in the morning as it goes creamier overnight.

³/₄ cup brown rice
3 cups water
pinch sea salt

▶ Wash brown rice and place in a pot with water and sea salt. Cook for 40 minutes on a medium to low heat.
▶ Leave overnight and have cool for breakfast or heat and serve.

WHEAT BISCUIT CEREAL ▶

Organic wheat-bix are fresh and crunchy.

2 apples
³/₄ cup water
3 wheat-bix
1 cup rice milk
1 teaspoon maple syrup

▶ Core apples and chop into chunks then cook with water for 10 minutes. Leave to cool.
▶ Place wheat-bix in a bowl with stewed apples, rice milk and maple syrup.

SCRAMBLED EGGS ▶

A power breakfast. Organic free-range chickens are fed on certified organic grains and run freely on the open farm.

3 eggs
1 tablespoon rice milk
pinch sea salt
¹/₄ cup spring onions
1¹/₂ tablespoons sesame oil
1 cup potato, sliced
1 tomato, sliced
¹/₂ cup mushrooms, sliced
1 avocado
1 teaspoon shoyu

▶ Mix eggs with rice milk and sea salt.
▶ Sauté spring onions in half tablespoon of sesame oil for 2 minutes then add eggs and stir for 2–3 minutes until scrambled.
▶ Boil potato for 5 minutes then fry in 1 tablespoon of sesame oil with tomato and mushrooms. Turn ingredients until both sides are crispy.
▶ Place scrambled eggs, potato, tomatoes and mushrooms on a plate with slices of avocado covered with shoyu.

SOUPS

MISO SOUP ▶

When you have miso soup before a meal it prepares your digestive system for food. Taken before bed it relaxes your liver, pancreas, spleen and kidneys. In the morning it stimulates activity and mental clarity. Because miso is so salty you must not have more than 10 bowls per week.

¹/₂ cup carrots, cut into fine matchsticks
2 cups water
¹/₂ cup wakame seaweed
2 teaspoons mugi miso

▶ Boil carrots in water for 3 minutes.
▶ Add wakame seaweed and miso mixed with a little cooking liquid and simmer for a further 2 minutes. Always mix miso paste into a liquid state before adding to soup, or it will become lumpy.
▶ Serve and enjoy.

MISO AND PUMPKIN SOUP ▶

Miso paste builds intestinal flora and strengthens the stomach and digestive system. It also detoxifies the colon.

¹/₂ cup pumpkin, cut into small cubes
3 cups water
¹/₂ cup wakame seaweed
1 tablespoon miso

▶ Boil pumpkin in water for 10 minutes.
▶ Wash wakame seaweed and add to pumpkin.
▶ Add miso mixed with a little cooking liquid and simmer for a further 2 minutes. Serve hot.

LEMON MISO SOUP ▶

Cauliflower has anti-cancer properties and with miso builds a powerful defence for body vitality.

¹/₂ cup cauliflower, small florets
3 cups water
¹/₄ cup arame seaweed
1 tablespoon miso
¹/₂ cup lemon slices

▶ Boil cauliflower in water for 5 minutes then add arame and miso paste mixed with a little cooking liquid.
▶ Simmer for a further 2 minutes. Place a lemon slice in each bowl for zing and serve.

DAIKON MISO SOUP ▶

Daikon is the grand fat dissolver. It is a powerful healing food and has been used throughout Asia for centuries in this capacity. Daikon helps heal congestion and fat accumulation and is powerful in eliminating fatty deposits. This soup is excellent for eliminating chemicals and toxins from the blood.

2 cups water
1 cup daikon, thinly sliced
$^1\!/_2$ cup spring onions, diagonally sliced
$^1\!/_4$ cup wakame seaweed, washed and sliced
2 teaspoons mugi miso

▶ Place water in a pot and bring to the boil. Add daikon and spring onions.
▶ Simmer for 3–5 minutes until vegetables are tender.
▶ Add wakame and simmer for a further 2 minutes.
▶ Reduce to a very low heat and season with miso mixed with a little cooking liquid. Simmer for 2 minutes more. Serve.

ONION MISO SOUP ▶

A sweet rich soup. Onions nurture the lymphatic system. They are the sweetest vegetable when sautéed and can be caramelised.

3 cups onions, cut into half moons
1 tablespoon sesame oil
3 cups water
1 teaspoon lemon zest, grated
1 tablespoon miso paste

▶ Sauté onions with sesame oil for 10 minutes, tossing regularly.
▶ Add water and bring to the boil.
▶ Add lemon zest and miso mixed with a little cooking liquid.
▶ Simmer for 5 minutes. Serve.

MISO SOUP WITH SPRING ONIONS ▶

Rich miso soup tastes great with the oil-sautéed spring onions.

$^1\!/_2$ cup spring onions, chopped
1 teaspoon sesame oil
$^1\!/_4$ cup wakame seaweed
2 cups water
2 teaspoons mugi miso

▶ Sauté spring onions in sesame oil for 5 minutes then add water and washed wakame.
▶ Mix mugi miso with a little of the soup liquid in a cup and add to the soup mixture. Simmer for a further 2 minutes. Serve.

AZUKI BEAN SOUP ▶

Azuki beans strengthen tired kidneys. As kidneys are responsible for eliminating toxins and fluids from the body, strong kidneys build power into body tone and help prevent fluid retention.

1 cup azuki beans
4 cups water
1 strip kombu seaweed
1 cup carrots, cut into irregular chunks
1 cup onions, diced
1 cup cauliflower florets
1 tablespoon miso paste

▶ Place azuki beans in a pot with kombu seaweed and water and leave to soak for 3–6 hours.
▶ Add vegetables to pot.
▶ Boil on a low heat for 2 hours with a lid on.
▶ Mix miso paste with a little water and add to soup. Simmer for a further 5 minutes. Serve hot.

CHICKPEA SOUP ▶

Curry powder is great to add heat to any dish as it has cleansing properties. It also helps to increase metabolic action.

³/₄ cup chickpeas
1 strip kombu seaweed
1 cup onion, finely sliced
3¹/₂ cups water
1 teaspoon curry powder
¹/₂ teaspoon sea salt
¹/₄ cup spring onions and/or parsley

▶ Soak chickpeas for 3–6 hours. Rinse and drain.
▶ Place soaked chickpeas, kombu seaweed and onions into a pressure-cooker or heavy pot. Cover with water and cook at medium heat for 1¹/₂ hours.
▶ Blend mixture into a smooth consistency and season with curry powder and sea salt. Simmer for a further 3 minutes.
▶ Serve garnished with spring onions and/or parsley.

QUICK LENTIL SOUP ▶

To save time you can use a can of lentils or leftovers from the night before.

1 cup onions, cut into half moons
1 cup celery, cut into diagonals
1 tablespoon sesame oil
1 cup water
1 can lentils or 2 cups cooked lentils
½ cup wakame seaweed, washed and cut into small pieces
1 tablespoon tamari
1 cup organic pasta — elbows, shells or noodles
¼ cup parsley

▶ Sauté onions and celery with sesame oil for 5 minutes. Add water and boil for 2–3 minutes.
▶ Add lentils, wakame and tamari and simmer for 3 minutes.
▶ In a separate pot, boil pasta for 10 minutes on a medium heat. Drain and place into a serving bowl.
▶ Pour soup over pasta and garnish with finely chopped parsley.

TOFU AND VEGETABLE SOUP ▶

So quick and easy, this soup offers perfect organic food balance.

3 cups water
½ cup arame seaweed
½ cup onions, diced
½ cup carrots, diced
½ block tofu, cut into small cubes
1 teaspoon sunflower oil
1 tablespoon shoyu
½ cup watercress

▶ Bring water to boil with arame seaweed and simmer on a low heat for 5 minutes.
▶ In another pan, stir-fry onions, carrots and tofu with sunflower oil for 5 minutes. Add this to the soup broth.
▶ Flavour the broth with shoyu and simmer for a further 5 minutes.
▶ Garnish with watercress. Serve.

PUMPKIN SOUP ▶

Pumpkin is thought to have originated in South America where it has been enjoyed for centuries.

2 cups buttercup pumpkin, cut into small chunks
3¹/₂ cups water
1 tablespoon mugi miso
¹/₂ cup spring onions, finely sliced
1 sheet toasted nori seaweed, cut into fine strips

▶ Place pumpkin in a pot with water. Bring to the boil, reduce to a low heat and simmer for 30 minutes. Blend, purée or mash pumpkin.
▶ Mix miso paste with hot water to liquefy and add to pumpkin soup. Stir into the soup gently and simmer for a further 5 minutes.
▶ Use spring onions and nori to garnish soup.

WATERCRESS, ONION AND CARROT BROTH WITH TOFU AND NOODLES ▶

A high-mineral broth – great for lunch or dinner.

³/₄ cup carrots, cut into matchsticks
¹/₂ block tofu, cut into cubes
3 cups water
¹/₂ cup hijiki seaweed
1 tablespoon miso
³/₄ cup watercress

▶ Add carrots, tofu and hijiki seaweed to water in pot and boil for 10 minutes.
▶ Mix miso paste into a liquid with a little soup water in a cup then add to broth with watercress and simmer for a further 3 minutes. Serve.

KOMBU VEGETABLE SOUP ▶

This soup is rich in minerals from the kombu seaweed, which adds strength to every cell. This offers resilience to organs and helps build tone deep within the body.

1¹/₂ cups carrots, cut into half moons
³/₄ cup broccoli florets
1 strip kombu seaweed
3 cups water
1 tablespoon miso

▶ Add carrots and broccoli to a pot with kombu and water.
▶ Bring to the boil and simmer with the lid on for 1 hour.
▶ Mix miso paste with a little water. Add to soup and simmer for a further 5 minutes. Serve.

BARLEY AND LENTIL SOUP ▶

Lentils increase metabolic action and help break down fat. Barley is known for its special healing qualities on the liver, so with a healthy liver and good metabolism – look out fat!

¹/₂ cup barley
¹/₂ cup lentils
1 strip kombu seaweed
¹/₂ cup pumpkin, chopped
¹/₂ cup carrots, chopped
¹/₂ cup potatoes, chopped
1 tablespoon fresh herbs
2 tablespoons tamari
1 tablespoon seed mustard

▶ Place all ingredients except tamari and mustard into a pot and simmer for 1¹/₂ hours. Blend to a fine consistency.
▶ Season with tamari and seed mustard. Serve.

FRENCH ONION SOUP ▶

Onions thin down the blood and are great fat dissolvers. They balance the fried bread in this soup. For a strong, cleansing soup serve this without the fried bread.

2 cups onions, cut into half moons
1 cup mushrooms, sliced
3 cups water
1 tablespoon tamari
2 tablespoons sesame oil
2 slices sourdough bread
¹/₄ cup spring onions, finely sliced

▶ Sauté onions for 3 minutes in half a cup of water until translucent. Add mushrooms and sauté for another 2 minutes.
▶ Add remaining water and bring to the boil. Cover the pot and simmer for 20 minutes. Season with tamari.
▶ Heat sesame oil in a frying pan and add bread cut into 3 cm cubes. Fry bread until golden brown. Remove bread and drain on a clean paper towel.
▶ Place soup in individual serving bowls and garnish each with several slices of fried bread cubes and spring onions.

FUEL FOOD – PASTA AND NOODLE DISHES

To cook noodles or pasta properly or 'al dente' – which means they should still be firm when bitten – you need to add pasta or noodles to a pot of rapidly boiling water.

After adding, stir noodles briefly, then, as the water returns to the boil, add 1 cup of cold water. Cook for about 4–12 minutes, depending on the size and thickness of the noodles and the heat of the water.

A properly cooked noodle should be the same colour right through. If the centre of the noodle or pasta is a different colour, then it is not properly cooked. To stop noodles over-cooking, simply drain and rinse under cold water.

UDON NOODLE, CARROT AND COURGETTE SAUTÉ ▶

Udon noodles are superior because the flour is kneaded, rolled, then cut into noodles, which gives a springy, alive quality.

1 packet udon noodles
1 tablespoon sesame oil
2 cloves garlic, diced
1 cup carrots, cut into matchsticks
1 cup courgettes, cut diagonally
1 tablespoon shoyu
1 tablespoon brown rice vinegar

▶ Boil udon noodles for 10–12 minutes.
▶ Heat sesame oil in frying pan.
▶ Stir-fry garlic for approximately 2 minutes or until transparent. Add carrots and courgettes and cook for a further 3 minutes.
▶ Add cooked udon noodles and shoyu. Sauté for 2 more minutes then add brown rice vinegar. Serve.

UDON WITH GREEN BEANS AND COURGETTES ▶

This simple udon dish goes well with greens for a lunch or a dinner when you are in the mood for quick, healthy food.

1 cup green beans, cut diagonally
³/₄ cup courgettes, cut into irregular chunks
1 packet cooked udon noodles
1 teaspoon flaxseed oil
1 teaspoon tamari
1 teaspoon brown rice vinegar
1 teaspoon sesame seaweed shake

▶ Blanch beans and courgettes and add to cooked udon noodles.
▶ Mix together all ingredients and serve hot or cold.

UDON NOODLES WITH SHITAKE MUSHROOMS ▶

Shitake mushrooms have healing properties and help rid the body of mucous congestion.

1 cup shitake mushrooms
1 tablespoon tamari
1 tablespoon sesame oil
½ cup onions, diced
1 cup cabbage, shredded
2 cups cooked udon noodles
¼ cup parsley

▶ Soak shitake mushrooms in water with ½ tablespoon tamari for 15 minutes then chop shitake into thin strips.
▶ Place shitake soaking liquid into frying pan with sesame oil and heat. Add onions and shitake mushrooms and sauté for 5 minutes.
▶ Add cabbage, cover and cook for a further 5 minutes.
▶ Add udon noodles and remaining tamari to mixture and cook for another 3 minutes, stirring occasionally. Garnish with parsley.

ONE POT UDON DISH ▶

Use any vegetable or pasta you like. I often make this dish when I'm dashing about and don't have a lot of time to cook.

1 packet udon noodles
1 cup broccoli, small florets
½ cup carrots, cut into small half moons
¾ cup leeks, finely sliced
½ block tofu, chopped into 3 cm blocks
1 tablespoon shoyu
1 tablespoon brown rice vinegar
1 tablespoon flaxseed oil

▶ Bring plenty of water to the boil and cook udon noodles for 5 minutes, then add vegetables and tofu. Cook for another 5 minutes, stirring occasionally.
▶ Rinse and drain then place on a plate. Season with shoyu, brown rice vinegar and flaxseed oil.

ELBOW PASTA AND TOFU WITH STEAMED GREENS ▶

Kids love this recipe.

1 cup elbow pasta
1 cup silverbeet or spinach
½ block tofu, cut in small cubes
1 teaspoon shoyu

▶ Boil elbow pasta for 8–10 minutes.
▶ Steam silverbeet or spinach with tofu. Drain then chop silverbeet or spinach finely.
▶ In a bowl mix elbow pasta, greens and tofu. Add shoyu and serve.

SOBA NOODLE SAUTÉ ▶

Soba noodles are made from buckwheat, which is the most effective fluid-absorbing grain, so this dish is ideal for reducing fluid retention.

1 packet soba noodles
1 tablespoon sunflower oil
$\frac{1}{2}$ cup carrots, cut into half moons
1 cup cabbage, sliced finely
1 tablespoon shoyu
1 tablespoon brown rice vinegar

▶ Boil soba noodles for 8–10 minutes.
▶ Heat sunflower oil in a frying pan and sauté carrots for 2 minutes. Add cabbage and sauté for a further 4 minutes.
▶ Add cooked soba noodles. Season with shoyu and brown rice vinegar and serve hot.

SOBA NOODLES WITH HIJIKI ▶

Hijiki is one of the richest sources of calcium. It primarily grows in the Far East and is harvested between January and May when its growth is at a peak. Hijiki will expand to up to 5 times its dry volume, so be careful not to soak it for too long.

$\frac{1}{4}$ cup hijiki seaweed
1 cup broccoli florets
1 tablespoon ginger root, sliced
1 tablespoon sesame oil
1 packet cooked soba noodles
1 tablespoon shoyu

▶ Soak hijiki for 10 minutes. Wash to remove any sand particles, then slice into 4 cm long pieces.
▶ Simmer hijiki in water with lid on pot for 5 minutes. Add broccoli and simmer for a further 3 minutes, then drain.
▶ Sauté ginger in sesame oil for 2 minutes then add hijiki, soba noodles, broccoli and shoyu. Sauté for 3 minutes and serve.

SOBA NOODLE AND TOFU STIR-FRY ▶

Cabbage is the best fluid-absorbing vegetable and soba, the best fluid-absorbing noodle. What a combination for sleek body form!

1 teaspoon sesame oil
1 cup cabbage, finely shredded
1 block tofu, cut into small cubes
2 cups cooked soba noodles
1 teaspoon tamari
1 teaspoon brown rice vinegar

▶ Heat sesame oil in a wok or frying pan and add cabbage.
▶ Toss for 3 minutes, then add tofu and sauté for a further 3 minutes.
▶ Add cooked soba noodles and tamari and heat through.
▶ Splash with brown rice vinegar and serve hot.

PENNE PASTA SAUTÉ ▶

A quick and easy dish.

³/₄ cup red capsicum, sliced
1 teaspoon sesame oil
2 cups cooked penne pasta
1 cup parsley, chopped finely
1 teaspoon shoyu
1 teaspoon brown rice vinegar
¹/₂ cup black olives

▶ Sauté capsicum in sesame oil for 3 minutes in a wok or frying pan, then add penne pasta and parsley.
▶ Flavour the mixture with shoyu and brown rice vinegar. Sauté for another 3 minutes.
▶ Place in bowl with olives on top. Serve.

TOFU AND SPAGHETTI SAUTÉ ▶

Tofu absorbs any flavour and in this dish the shoyu and brown rice vinegar marinade provide the flavour.

1 block tofu, sliced into 1 cm pieces
1 tablespoon shoyu
1 teaspoon brown rice vinegar
1 tablespoon sesame oil
2 cloves garlic, diced
1 cup onions, cut into half moons
¹/₂ cup snow peas
2 cups cooked spaghetti
1 cup mung bean sprouts

▶ Marinate tofu with shoyu and brown rice vinegar for ¹/₂ hour. Retain marinade.
▶ Heat sesame oil in a wok or frying pan and sauté garlic and onions until transparent.
▶ Add tofu and snow peas and sauté for a further 3 minutes.
▶ Add spaghetti and mung bean sprouts and heat through for 3 more minutes.
▶ Season with shoyu and brown rice vinegar marinade. Serve.

VEGETABLE AND TOFU KEBABS ▶

Great for barbecues and outdoor eating.

2 blocks tofu, cut into 2 cm cubes
1 tablespoon tamari
1 cup kumara, sliced into rounds
1 cup carrots, sliced into rounds
1 cup pumpkin, cut into 2 cm cubes
1 cup capsicum, cut into irregular pieces
1 cup onion, quartered
5 wooden skewers

▶ Marinate tofu in tamari for 15–30 minutes.
▶ Boil kumara, carrots and pumpkin for 3 minutes then drain.
▶ Spike all ingredients onto wooden skewers and cook on barbecue for about 5 minutes, rotating often.

NOODLE AND ARAME SAUTÉ ▶

A rich, wholesome dish, this stir-fry is a simple meal that provides carbohydrates, minerals and protein.

$\frac{1}{2}$ cup arame seaweed soaked in water for 10 minutes
1 tablespoon sunflower oil
1 cup spring onions, finely sliced on a diagonal
4 cloves garlic, diced
2 cups cooked noodles
2 cups exotic tonic greens, sliced coarsely
1 tablespoon tamari
1 tablespoon brown rice vinegar

▶ Heat sunflower oil in frying pan and add spring onions and garlic, tossing for 3 minutes. Drain arame seaweed and add to the mixture with cooked noodles. Cook for a further 3 minutes.
▶ Add exotic tonic greens and cook for 2 more minutes.
▶ Splash mixture with tamari and brown rice vinegar and heat through for 2 minutes before serving.

RICE PASTA WITH BAKED BEANS ▶

A quick dish using organic baked beans, which are a brilliant source of protein.

2 cups cooked rice pasta
1 can baked beans
$\frac{1}{2}$ cup spring onions, finely sliced
1 teaspoon shoyu

▶ Heat baked beans, spring onions and shoyu for 5 minutes.
▶ Pour baked bean mixture over rice pasta and eat hot.

DESSERTS

APPLE DESSERT ▶

Raisins are dried white grapes — they darken as they dry. Currants are dried from a variety of red grape.

3 cups apples, peeled, cored and chopped
1 teaspoon lemon zest, sliced into matchslicks
1 tablespoon raisins
2 cups water

▶ Boil all ingredients for 30 minutes with lid on.
▶ Serve mixture hot. You may wish to add maple syrup or rice malt to sweeten this dessert and can enjoy it with either soy milk or rice milk for richness and flavour.

APPLE AND PEAR PURÉE ▶

Sweet and juicy.

2 cups apples, cored and chopped
2 cups pears, cored and chopped
2 cups water

▶ Cook apples and pears in water for half an hour. Allow to cool.
▶ Add yoghurt or rice milk to flavour.

BAKED APPLES ▶

Sultanas are dried seedless white grapes.

3 apples
$\frac{1}{2}$ cup sultanas
$\frac{1}{2}$ cup yoghurt

▶ Core apples and fill with sultanas.
▶ Bake in a 200°C oven for 30–40 minutes.
▶ Serve with yoghurt.

MILLET DESSERT ◗

A sweet and tender dessert. Try adding yoghurt or cream if you feel like a richer dessert. This can also be eaten as a snack or breakfast cereal.

1 cup millet cereal
pinch sea salt
3 cups rice milk
1 teaspoon brown rice malt or honey
1 teaspoon apricot jam

◗ Mix together millet cereal, sea salt and rice milk and bring to the boil. Simmer for 5 minutes, stirring regularly to avoid lumps forming.
◗ Place in a serving bowl and allow to cool for a few minutes, which gives a lovely skin on top. Add brown rice malt or honey and apricot jam.

COUSCOUS CAKE ◗

So easy and yet so good, couscous is made from wheat and is delicious made into a cake.

1¹⁄₂ cups couscous
pinch salt
¹⁄₂ cup raisins
2¹⁄₄ cups water
2 tablespoons strawberry jam

◗ Dry-roast couscous in frying pan until golden to give a nutty flavour to the cake – this should take around 2–3 minutes.
◗ Add salt, raisins and couscous to water and simmer with lid on for 10 minutes.
◗ Turn heat off and leave for 10 minutes then place in cake tin and allow to set for half an hour.
◗ Remove and spread with strawberry jam. Serve cold.

RAISIN DESSERT ◗

Millet cereal made with vanilla rice milk is delicious and creamy as a dessert.

¹⁄₂ cup raisins
Pinch sea salt
1 cup water
³⁄₄ cup millet cereal
2¹⁄₂ cups vanilla rice milk

◗ Cook raisins and sea salt in water for 30 minutes and then blend in a food processor.
◗ Heat millet cereal and vanilla rice milk with a pinch of sea salt until creamy. Allow to cool.
◗ Place millet cereal in a bowl and serve with raisin purée on top.

RESOURCE DIRECTORY

RETAILERS

Arcadia Organics/Healthy Hog Café
265 High Street, Motueka
Phone/fax (03) 528 7840
email: arcadia-@ihug.co.nz
http://homepages.ihug.co.nz/~marahau/

Back to Eden
219 Old Taupo Road, Rotorua
Phone (07) 348 8302
Fax (07) 348 1503
email: norriss@wave.co.nz

Bethlehem Health Shop
SH 2, Tauranga
Phone (07) 576 9442
Fax (07) 548 1933

BioShop
Shop 4, Opawa Mall, 124 Opawa Road,
Christchurch
Phone (03) 337 0022
Fax (03) 384 6521

Brownowl Organic and Natural Products
557 Waitarere Beach Road, Levin
Phone (06) 368 4451
Fax (06) 326 5555
email: jillb@clear.net.nz

Ceres Enlivening Products
181 Ladies Mile, Ellerslie, Auckland
Phone (09) 579 7126
Fax (09) 525 5509

Chantal Foods
45 Hastings Street, Napier
Phone (06) 835 8036
Fax (06) 835 7018

Clark's Organic Butchery
356 West Coast Road, Glen Eden, Auckland
Phone (09) 818 6526
Fax (09) 818 6592

Clean GreeNZ Organics
25 Rose Street, Blenheim
Phone (03) 577 9494

Commonsense Organics
260 Wakefield Street, Wellington
Phone (04) 384 3314
Fax (04) 385 3383
email: kebwood@xtra.co.nz

Down to Earth
268 Devon Street West, New Plymouth
Phone/fax (06) 758 3700

Earthfoods Organic NZ Propriety Ltd
27 Tennyson St, Napier
Phone (06) 835 5787
Fax (06)835 4116
www.earthfoods.co.nz

Earth Seed Organics
547–549 West Coast Road, Oratia, Auckland
Phone/fax (09) 818 6411
email: steveed@kiwilink.co.nz

East West Organics
374 West Coast Road, Glen Eden, Auckland
Phone (09) 818 9524
Fax (09) 818 2903
email: eastwest.organics@clear.net.nz

Good Earth
1046 Cameron Road, Tauranga
Phone/fax (07) 578 7211

Harvest Whole Foods
403–405 Richmond Road, Grey Lynn, Auckland
Phone (09) 376 3107
Fax (09) 360 1616

Harvest Organics Devonport
26 Clarence Street, Devonport
Phone (09) 446 0100
Fax (09) 446 0101

Healthy Organics
313 Barton Street, Hamilton
PO Box 689, Hamilton
Phone (07) 838 9932
Fax (07) 838 9942

Homestead Health Foods
112 Cuba Mall, Cuba Street, Wellington
Phone (04) 802 4425
Fax (04) 802 4426
email: hshealth@clear.net.nz

Huckleberry Farms
240 Greenlane Road West, Epsom, Auckland
Phone (09) 630 8857

I.E. Produce
1 Barry's Point Road, Takapuna, Auckland
Phone (09) 488 0211

Invercargill Organic Shop
329 North Road, Waikiwi, Invercargill
Phone (03) 215 7415

It's Healthy
The Plaza, Kaitaia
Phone (09) 408 2606
Fax (09) 408 3719

Kelmarna Organic City Farm
12 Hukunui Cres, Herne Bay, Auckland
Phone/fax (09) 376 0472
email: kelmarna@framework.org.nz
www.http//:framework.org.nz

Linda's Organics
253 Oxford Street, Levin
Phone/fax (06) 367 5997
www.kiwiconnect.co.nz/organics/linda'sorganic's

Made in Nippon
478 Queen Street, Auckland Central
Phone (09) 377 1891

Mamata Bakehouse
401 Richmond Road, Grey Lynn, Auckland
Phone (09) 376 3191

Natures Abundance
Unit 5, 300 Colombo Street, Sydenham, Christchurch
Phone (03) 332 3060
Fax (03) 332 5060
email: farm@pl.net

Opawa Bio Shop
124 Opawa Road, Christchurch
Phone (03) 337 0022
Fax (03) 384 6521

Organic Living
Broadtop Shopping Centre, Palmerston North
Phone (06) 353 0549

Organics Organics Shop
425 Cashel Street, Christchurch 1
Phone/fax (03) 381 1122

Organic World
181 Pt Chevalier Road, Pt Chevalier, Auckland
Phone (09) 845 3249
Fax(09) 845 3247
email: nicrai@xtra.co.nz

Piko Wholefoods Co-operatives
229 Kilmore Street, Christchurch 1
Phone (03) 366 8116
Fax (03) 366 8114
email: pikoshop@ihug.co.nz

The Good Earth
1046 Cameron Road, Gate Pa, Tauranga
Phone (07) 578 7211

The Green Grocer
40 Tasman Street, Nelson
Phone/fax (03) 548 3650

The Organic Store
5 Mangorei Road, New Plymouth
Phone (06) 759 9116
Fax (06) 759 9107

Torbay Fruit Shop
1034 Beach Road, Torbay, Auckland
Phone (09) 473 9429

Wah Lee
214–220 Hobson Street, Auckland Central
Phone (09) 373 4583

Waiheke Organic Food
20 Tahi Road, Ostend, Waiheke Island
Phone/fax (09) 372 8708

Waihi Beach Natural Health
31B Wilson Road, Waihi Beach
Phone/fax (07) 863 4350

West Lynn Meats
440 Richmond Road, Grey Lynn, Auckland
Phone (09) 376 1439

ORGANIC ASSOCIATIONS

Bio-Dynamic Farming and Gardening Association in NZ Incorporated
PO Box 39045, Wellington Mail Centre
Phone (04) 589 5366
Fax (04) 589 5365
email: biodynamics@clear.net.nz

BIO-GRO New Zealand
PO Box 9693, Marion Square, Wellington 6031
Phone (04) 801 9741
Fax (04) 801 9742

Soil & Health Association of New Zealand
PO Box 36170, Northcote, Auckland 9
Phone/fax (09) 480 4440

HOME DELIVERY

Organic Home Delivery
PO Box 1428, Auckland
Phone (09) 624 4220
Fax (09) 624 4223
email: sales@organicfoods.co.nz
www.organicfoods.co.nz

INDEX